Blessings in the Book of Revelation—Seen as a Play

by
Katie Snyder

Contents

Chapter 1
We Need to Understand Revelation

The book of Revelation is receiving a lot of attention these days and rightly so. For many reasons people are taking a closer look at it, despite its having been controversial in Christian circles since it was written. Some of the things mentioned in prophecy which for years have seemed outlandish are now possible. In 1948, the nation of Israel was created, and in 1967 the Jews regained control of the Old City in Jerusalem. Modern knowledge of earth science and the cosmos, not to mention communication and computer technology, have produced information and advancements that make some of the things that once seemed wondrous in Revelation actually commonplace and familiar. Of course, there will also be miraculous events beyond any explanation.

Despite recent books and even movies about prophecy, most lay believers are reluctant to probe Revelation's depths because of its complexity. Saying that Revelation is confusing is putting it mildly. After much frustration, I finally decided to undertake a comprehensive study of the book rather than sit through another Revelation Bible study. Of course, I examined what today's theologians said, but I found that none of them had a monopoly on the truth. Most of the theories they put forward are polemic discourses aimed at convincing us to buy into their logic. I wanted to see Revelation from a biblical perspective without a denominational bias.

That said, there is at least a modicum of scriptural support for most of the prevailing theories, but not one of them is totally convincing. As a testament to the difficulty theologians have had as they tried to make sense of a very perplexing book, some of them actually rely on the absence of a word to prove a point. All of them make assumptions that amount to gigantic leaps of faith, while they conveniently ignore other pertinent verses of Scripture. I realize that our Creator may have intended for prophecy to be cloaked in mystery but I'm also certain that He wants us to know and understand it. He very clearly said so.

There are blessings throughout the Scriptures but Revelation is the only book in the Bible actually containing a specific blessing for reading it. It's repeated twice, once at the beginning and again at the end. This is the reason that I believe Revelation should be the first step toward studying biblical prophecy. Though not easy to do, Revelation *can* be broken down and understood by anyone, not just the academic elite. So, Revelation's blessings are for everyone.

The information contained in these pages can be considered a primer for unlocking what I believe is the most important book of prophecy, even the foundation for understanding the rest of prophecy. My goals are to simplify and clarify, and to create a framework upon which anyone can build with further study. This is not a verse-by-verse or even chapter-by-chapter study. But hopefully it will be a tool for beginning a thorough exploration of Revelation and related prophecy.

My fervent desire is that you find this information helpful and will no longer be intimidated, as I once was, and will go on to study all prophecy further. I will be most gratified if this information is the first step in your exciting journey to better understand His Truth concerning the future.

Three principles guide my thinking. First, at certain times it will be expedient to go with a prevailing theory or to choose the easiest one if it makes sense and helps to clarify or simplify. The first step is to develop an appreciation for the basic facts.

Second, I skim over certain parts of Revelation because at this juncture they're not essential in our quest to understand the basics, or because the information is so complex that it's too distracting. The topics and issues not addressed in these pages can be fertile ground for later study.

Third, I don't agonize over whether something is literal or symbolic unless it helps in some way. That tends to lead down rabbit trails that seem to have no end. Theologians may disagree vehemently on this point, but the evidence suggests that they haven't been all that successful in helping people understand Revelation. My approach might be of value for some people, even if not for all.

In Matthew 24:32 the Messiah urges watching for the tender leaves on the tree—the signs of coming events. So it's very important to be familiar with the basic facts that form the overall framework for prophecy. But we also need to know as many details as possible, realizing of course that we will have to fill in some gaps as things unfold. I believe that it's impossible to develop a comprehensive understanding of these future events before they even begin. Yet, we are responsible for being informed.

Time, though, is of the essence. Revelation 1: 3 says that the time is short/quick/near, depending on the translation. If translated as "quick" or "short", it becomes more important to understand Revelation and related prophecy before things start unfolding. There may not be enough time for thorough Bible study once certain events are set into motion. Like birth pangs, the pains increase rapidly.

The danger in being wholeheartedly sold on any one theory is not recognizing something important when it happens and becoming confused when events don't turn out the way you expected. Isaiah 28:15b says, "For we have made falsehood our refuge and we have concealed ourselves with deception." Don't allow a popular theory to become a delusional refuge. The Messiah did not conform to prevailing expectations 2000 years ago, so He was rejected by the majority of the religious leaders of His day. Preconceived notions can prevent us from clearly seeing the truth.

Any theologian who is intellectually honest should be willing to admit that his theory can't be proven and he can't guarantee that events will unfold exactly the way he proposes. Rather than buy completely into any one position, be your own researcher. Each of us needs to study Revelation independently so the Heavenly Father can bless us with His understanding through the Holy Spirit.

Scripture is our weapon against the "thief in the night" mentioned in Revelation 3: 3. It prevents us from falling prey to false teaching, well-intentioned or not. We need to study Revelation and other prophecy so we will not be surprised, as unbelievers will be, when God's plan comes to fruition. We may not understand everything perfectly, but we will know what is necessary at that time.

Chapter 2
Look at Revelation as a Play

When the Messiah walked the earth and taught, He mentioned two ages—this present age and the one to come. (Matt. 12:32) He taught about the coming kingdom, often using parables to give information, instruction and warnings about the end of days. Most people just read over these areas quickly, focusing instead on His more concrete and more easily understood teachings. But after studying Revelation, scripture elsewhere that pertains to prophecy and the future kingdom will become more noticeable and clearer. Even well-known passages such as the Lord's Prayer or the 23rd Psalm will take on more significance and have a deeper meaning. The blessings just continue to flow.

Revelation itself hints at how to divide it – "things…seen, and the things which are, and the things which shall take place after these things." (Rev.1:19) In other words, past and present and future. Most scholars agree that Revelation 1's vision of the Son of Man, the Messiah, is what John had "seen." The seven letters to the seven churches in Revelation 2 and 3 make up "the things which are." Revelation 4 through 22 is the vision of future events in the last days. This interpretation is plausible and helps clarify.

Before jumping into Revelation, it is best to understand why these events have to take place. What has brought mankind to this point? Well, it's no accident that Genesis and Revelation are the two "bookends" of the Bible. (Ray Stedman) The events of Revelation are directly connected to Adam and Eve. The Heavenly Father has a plan to usher in His perfect kingdom through the events outlined in Revelation and also seen in prophecy sprinkled generously throughout the Old and New Testaments.

The Messiah's first coming to earth was to give Himself as the provision for our sins, sin whose roots are in the Garden of Eden. His Second Coming will usher in a kingdom that will replace the earthly kingdom of sin. He will reclaim His rightful reign over earth. (Robert Van Campen) His new kingdom may well be another "Garden of Eden." Isaiah 4:5-6 describes Mt. Zion as a place of shelter, refuge and protection in the future. It is important to understand that the violent and even horrific events of Revelation will give way to an idyllic existence of no sorrow or pain, and a close fellowship with our Creator, in a beautiful setting. I Corinthians 2:9 says that "eye has not seen and ear has not heard…all that God has prepared for those who love Him."

Another possible reason is revealed in Isaiah 2:2. "In the last days, the mountain of the house of the Lord will be established as the chief of the mountains, and it will be raised above the hills; and all the nations will stream to it." So if Jerusalem will be the earth's highest point, all the rest will have to be lowered, maybe even leveled.

It is difficult to decipher prophecy even when one comprehends the words. Understanding *what* is being described is the first step, though. There are many ways to reach that goal. I share with you the way that I came to understand it.

In the same manner that the Messiah used common analogies in His parables which people could easily relate to, viewing Revelation as a play helps to break it up so as to be better understood. Familiar to most people, plays often have action and interludes. Unlike most plays, Revelation has many interludes and some are very long. The action in Revelation is dominated by three well-known series of judgments – seals (Revelation 6), trumpets (Revelation 8 and 9) and bowls (Revelation 16). Many theories abound as to their meaning and their relationship to each other. For the sake of simplicity, consider the seal judgments to be the overview, or a preview in the sense of foreshadowing coming events. They could even be a broad description of the overall consequences of the following trumpet and bowl judgments.

The trumpet judgments are those affecting one-third of the earth. They seem to be localized while the more devastating bowl judgments clearly affect the entire earth. Whether all of these judgments occur sequentially or simultaneously is the subject of multiple theories. A preliminary step is to look at them separately and later decide how they might intersect. There is additional action after the three series of judgments when the Millennial Kingdom ushers in the New Heaven and New Earth.

The interludes are even less clearly understood, and are the subject of diverse interesting interpretations. To simply know the information contained in them is a primary goal, and they could be easier than one might think. Consider the following. Some interludes serve as preludes to action, to prepare for the action. One interlude is like an aside in a play, where the narrator speaks directly to the audience. Lastly, other interludes are informational, giving background so as to better understand the action. For the sake of simplicity and clarity, it helps to separate the interludes from each other and from the action initially. Once studied, they merge together much more smoothly.

Plays usually have various settings, characters, props and costumes. Revelation contains these as well. Details concerning them will be mentioned as will a few other areas unrelated to plays but worthy of attention: blessings, promises, praise, questions, commands and warnings.

Since there is a dire warning (Rev. 22:18-19) against adding to or taking away from the words of Revelation, consider this dissecting of the different parts to be only temporary. All scripture is our Heavenly Father's holy word, despite the unfortunate translation errors that have occurred and still exist. Believers have a responsibility to try to understand even the complex to the best of their ability.

The one overriding message in Revelation and all prophecy is that Our Creator is sovereign. This is clear in every chapter and almost every verse of Revelation. The Creator of each unique individual and all that our eyes can see, and more, holds the entire universe in His hands. We need only to turn to Him and His word and obey. The most oft repeated phrase of Revelation is, "He who has an ear, let him hear what the Spirit says to the churches."

Chapter 3
Overview of the "Play"

The first order of business is to look at the author. The originator or creator of the words of Revelation is our Heavenly Father who gives His Son the very important message about the future Second Coming. The Messiah then shares this information with believers by way of an angel who shows John all that he is to write down for the churches to hear and heed. Revelation 1:4-5 indicates that Revelation's message is from the Father, the Son and the Holy Spirit. Their message is of utmost importance.

Initially, it is best not to worry about the timing of events or their exact length. That can come later because much of the information for this is in Old Testament and New Testament prophecy outside of Revelation, and it's quite complex. The first priority is to understand the "what," "where" and "who" before delving into the "when." The "when" has caused the most disagreement and controversy among scholars. Taking a cue from the New Testament's most important block of scripture on prophecy besides Revelation, Matthew 24, the "when" is answered in a roundabout way. The disciples ask the Messiah three questions. "Tell us, when will these things be, and what will be the sign of Your coming, and of the end of the age?" (vs. 3) He answers the two "what" questions and the "when" question by referring to preliminary events, "the beginning of birth pangs," which constitute "what" information. One could postulate that knowing the "what" helps to know the "when."

As for the "where," there are two main settings – heaven and earth. Also mentioned are mid-heaven and the abyss, which is evidently distinct from the lake of fire. In addition, at the end of Revelation, the New Heaven and New Earth replace the old ones.

As for the "what," most theories agree that a tribulation period of seal judgments, trumpet judgments and bowl judgments precede the second coming of Messiah and His Millennial Kingdom for one thousand years, followed by the New Heaven and New Earth. There is also a lot of "what" information in Isaiah and other Old Testament prophecy that can be added later to one's Revelation knowledge.

The characters or the "who" are difficult to separate from the "what." Both the action and the interludes include various humans, angels and other beings, some very unfamiliar yet fascinating. The goal is to know the general "story" and the "characters" so well that the complex details can be better managed.

A helpful tactic is to consider what may be a pattern used at times in Scripture: giving an overview before going into detail, usually where there appears to be repetition. Repetition is also used for emphasis, in summaries and for poetic purposes. Nevertheless, using this biblical teaching principle, which is also a common instructional tool, a summary overview will precede the more detailed chapter-by-chapter overview.

Summary Overview

Revelation is John's description of the future that involves the return of the Messiah. It begins with a salutation followed by a vision of the risen Messiah in all His glory. Then the seven letters to the seven churches give praise to the Messiah and advice to the churches and, by extension, to all believers. There is a heavenly vision of the Father on His throne, surrounded by praise from twenty-four elders and four living creatures. Then the Messiah takes a scroll, or book, which is sealed. As He begins to open the seals of the scroll, judgments are unleashed on earth, ranging from natural disasters to war. Next, a vision of heaven introduces the 144,000 and the tribulation saints. This is followed by the trumpet judgments that affect one-third of the earth, again ranging from natural disasters to war. A series of different visions (interludes), some in heaven and some on earth, precede a description of the final bowl judgments, which are worldwide in scope. This is followed by an interlude description of the global conditions in the last days. Ultimately, the triumphal return of the Messiah ushers in the Millennial Kingdom, which is followed by the New Heaven and New Earth.

Chapter-by-chapter Overview

Revelation 1 is an introduction. It begins with a salutation, in the midst of which a blessing is given to he who reads, hears and heeds the prophecy of Revelation. John beholds a wondrous vision of "one like a son of Man," the Messiah. He falls at His feet but is told not to fear. John is then instructed to write what he sees.

Revelation 2 and 3 are the letters written to seven churches outside Israel. They contain a seven-fold pattern of commission, character, commendation, condemnation, correction, call and challenge. (Ed Hindson) Some scholars see these letters as a picture of church history, while others see them as a picture of different types of churches, possibly on a continuum from most faithful to dead with varying degrees of compromise in the middle. They could also be a picture of different types of people in churches throughout time. Why couldn't it also include insight into every individual, who not only can have these various qualities but can go through different periods in their spiritual growth? It would be typical of our omniscient Creator to make the section that appears to be easiest to understand actually complex beyond a cursory reading. Maybe it's all of the above or some mixture therein. It's interesting to contemplate all of the possibilities. The bottom line is that every believer should heed the admonitions and advice in the letters to the churches. No believer should think he or she is exempt.

Revelation 4 and 5 together form an interlude describing a majestic view of heaven, which seems to serve as a prelude to the seal judgments. The Heavenly Father's throne is surrounded by twenty-four elders and four living creatures who are worshiping Him. A slain Lamb standing before the throne takes a book (scroll) with seven seals from His right hand. The rejoicing four living creatures and twenty-four elders sing a new song, while myriads of angels join in praising the Lamb who is "worthy…to take the book and break its seals."

Revelation 6 is an action chapter that presents six of the seven seal judgments. (The seventh seal is opened in Revelation 8.) The six seals are described in more general terms than the later trumpet and bowl judgments. Another thing that sets the seal judgments apart is that the first four reveal the well-known four horsemen of the apocalypse who cause political and economic turmoil. An additional distinction is that the fifth seal concerns the martyred souls crying out for justice, something unseen in the trumpets or bowls. On the other hand, the sixth seal results in geologic and cosmic disturbances that are quite similar to those described in the trumpets and bowls. Again, these seal judgments possibly give a preview, an overview or a summary of the overall consequences of the coming trumpet and bowl judgments.

Revelation 7 is a heavenly interlude describing the 144,000 who must be sealed and the great multitude who "come out of the great tribulation," tribulation saints. There are different explanations on these groups. What is certain is that the 144,000 are from the twelve Hebrew tribes, although the different lists of the tribes vary slightly throughout the Bible. The great multitude is from "every nation and all tribes and peoples and tongues." All are praising the Heavenly Father.

Revelation 8 and 9 include the trumpet judgments—back to action, but only after a short pause. The seventh seal is broken and three prelude events to the one-third judgments follow. First, a half hour of silence in heaven is succeeded by prayer using incense and then there is what can be considered a call to attention using thunder and lightning and an earthquake. In Revelation 8, the first four of the six trumpet judgments cause the destruction of one-third of the earth's vegetation, contamination of one-third of the earth's salt and fresh waters, destruction of one-third of all ships and sea creatures and the darkening of one-third of the sun and moon and stars.

Revelation 9 contains the fifth and sixth trumpet judgments, which are also called the first and second woes. (The third woe is the seventh trumpet.) The fifth trumpet (first woe) unleashes locusts "that torment only unbelievers for five months but do not harm believers" or any green thing. The sixth trumpet (second woe) involves armies of horsemen, 200 million strong, who kill one-third of mankind with plagues of fire and smoke and brimstone –possibly a nuclear holocaust?

Revelation 10 is another interlude open to many interpretations. Two angels come down from heaven, one standing on land and one on the sea. The angel standing on land has a little book open in his hand. As John is about to write, he is instructed to "seal up the things which the seven peals of thunder have spoken and do not write them." Then a voice from heaven tells John to eat the book which is sweet in his mouth but bitter in his stomach. This chapter is more like an aside because John is so involved. It is also very mysterious.

Revelation 11 begins with a continuation of the aside because John is instructed to measure the temple. Abruptly, the events change to a time at some point during the seal, trumpet and/or bowl judgments. Two witnesses with great powers prophesy for 3 ½ years in Jerusalem, are killed and are raised up to heaven after their bodies lie in the street for 3 ½ days. A great earthquake destroys a tenth of the city and 7000 people are killed.

Revelation 12 and 13 also have events that are difficult to place in a chronological slot. Additionally, these interludes are subject to great debate. In Revelation 12, a "woman with child" is pursued by a "great red dragon." She flees into the wilderness for 3 ½ years. There is war in heaven when Michael and his angels throw Satan to earth. Satan then persecutes "the woman who gave birth to the male child." She is flown into the wilderness on "the wings of the great eagle." The serpent (Satan/dragon) sends flood water after the woman but the earth swallows it.

In Revelation 13, "a beast coming up out of the sea" speaking blasphemies is worshiped by all unbelievers. A second beast "coming up out of the earth" attempts to make everyone worship the first beast. The second beast performs great signs and gives the mark of 666 on one's forehead or right hand for the purpose of buying and selling. Most agree that these two beasts are the antichrist and the false prophet.

Revelation 14 and 15 together are a prelude to the horrific bowl judgments of Revelation 16. In Revelation 14 the 144,000 sing a new song prior to angels bringing the gospel, a proclamation and an ultimatum. Then, angels of judgment reap a bloody harvest. The interpretations for this can be endless. In Revelation 15 John sees another sign in heaven, specifically described as "the wrath of God," in which seven angels have "seven plagues, which are the last." Victorious saints singing praises of the Heavenly Father precede these seven angels receiving "seven golden bowls full of the wrath of

God," and then the temple in heaven fills with smoke due to His glory and power.

Revelation 16 contains the final and most severe judgments, the bowls or plagues as they are also called. Some scholars see a significant distinction between the trumpet and bowl judgments: the trumpet or one-third judgments are viewed as Satan's persecution of believers through the antichrist and false prophet, whereas the worldwide bowl judgments are Yahweh's righteous wrath heaped upon the unbelieving world. Or it could be that the one-third trumpets are Yahweh's attempt to draw the world to Himself (trumpets are used for warning) and the bowls are His wrath poured out worldwide on those who do not repent.

It does help to differentiate between them in some manner. These bowl judgments devastate the earth and culminate in armies gathering at Armageddon. The first five bowls involve divine wrath, using natural disasters or diseases (plagues). But, like the sixth trumpet, the sixth bowl involves armies of men. Then the seventh bowl unleashes, with lightning and thunder, an earthquake unlike any other in human history. Not only are cities destroyed but islands and mountains are leveled, followed by 100-pound hailstones. Wow! Why does our Heavenly Father do this? Just remember that He is sovereign. The destruction is probably necessary in order to make way for His New Kingdom. Isaiah 24 and 25, as well as other scripture, describe this.

Revelation 17 and 18 together are an anticlimactic interlude of the informational type that seems to explain the world conditions during the end of days. Like the other interludes, much has to be interpreted. It helps to see it, and many agree, as a description of the fall of a worldwide religion and the fall of a global government. As in the Old Testament, the false religion is referred to as a "harlot" and ultimately will be destroyed, as will the global government and the leaders of each.

Revelation 19 and 20 describe the final action scenes. In Revelation 19 after great praise, preparations are underway for a marriage supper between Messiah the Lamb and His bride, the body of believers. Then the Messiah departs from heaven on a white horse with His heavenly armies to defeat His enemies, to rule and to judge on earth. Unfortunately, there is a feast for the birds from mid-heaven of dead bodies from this war. Lastly, the antichrist and the false prophet are thrown into the lake of fire. But that still leaves Satan.

Revelation 20 reveals the Millennial Kingdom, as Satan is bound for 1000 years in the abyss. The saints are resurrected. Then, Satan is released to deceive the nations for one last war. Thankfully, the Almighty El Shaddai devours with fire from heaven the armies out to destroy Jerusalem and the saints. Then Satan is thrown into the lake of fire with the beast and false prophet. Lastly, the infamous Great White Throne judgment judges everyone "according to their deeds." Maybe the Millennial Kingdom of Revelation 20 is a prelude to what's next.

In Revelation 21 a New Heaven and New Earth include a New Jerusalem in the eternal kingdom of no sorrow and no pain. There is complete satisfaction, full inheritance and close fellowship in a most exquisite setting.

Revelation 22 contains several parts that serve as an epilogue. A vision of heaven is followed by promises, a blessing for heeding the words of Revelation and three invitations to "come." But it also includes instruction and warnings. Ultimately, though, after death and destruction as well as judgment, paradise is restored!

In summary, the three series of judgments are followed by the Millennial Kingdom and the New Heaven and New Earth. The series of judgments (seals, trumpets, bowls), often referred to as the tribulation, is where it gets tricky. Incorporated into this series is seven years divided in half with two periods of 3 ½ years each. The second half is generally considered to be the great tribulation. Somewhere it is cut short. (Matt. 24:22) To be any more detailed than that is to wade into the muck, especially concerning when the rapture and the day of the Lord occur.

Chapter 4
Settings of the "Play"

As mentioned before, the two main settings are heaven and earth, though reference is made to other locations. Surprisingly there is as much information described about heaven as there is about earth in Revelation. It is one of the best scriptural sources for information on heaven, with back and forth interaction between heaven and earth throughout. John is transported to heaven spiritually in a vision which he is able to recount. It seems similar to what is described in Ezekiel 8:3.

Although the appearance of the Messiah in Revelation 1:12-20 is a heavenly vision, it is not clear where it occurred. The English translation indicates that John, on the island of Patmos (vs. 9), was "in the Spirit" (vs. 10) when he turned and saw (vs. 12) the Messiah in His glorified state. After the letters to the churches on earth in Revelation 2 and 3, Revelation 4 opens with a voice from heaven inviting John to "come up here." Clearly at this time John leaves earth to ascend to heaven in the spirit.

The entirety of Revelation 4 and 5 takes place in heaven. In Revelation 4, verse 2 says that "a throne was standing in heaven." After a detailed description of the Heavenly Father, His throne and

its surroundings, including twenty-four elders and four living
creatures, the continual heavenly praise is described. Revelation 5:3
not only mentions heaven but may actually be a guide for the various
settings of Revelation, that is, "in heaven, or on the earth or under the
earth." All of Revelation 5 takes place in heaven as activity around
the throne is described.

After Revelation 6's description of the seal judgments on earth,
Revelation 7 introduces the 144,000 on earth and the great multitude
of tribulation saints in heaven. John can see earth, as indicated in
verse 1, presumably from heaven. Verses 9 through 17 make
reference to the throne, angels, elders and the Lamb.

Revelation 8:1-5 describes the heavenly prelude of a half hour
of silence, prayer with incense and a call to attention of thunder,
lightning and an earthquake. The remainder of Revelation 8 and all
of Revelation 9 deal with the one-third trumpet judgments on earth.
Verse 13 mentions "an eagle flying in mid-heaven" who announces
the three woes of the remaining blasts of the trumpets.

Revelation 10 is interesting because it is more of an aside than a
regular interlude since it involves the writer/scribe, John, who is
given a little book to eat. Verse 1 indicates that an angel was "coming
down out of heaven." Then verse 8 says "the voice which I heard
from heaven." These two verses suggest that John was on earth but
was interacting with heavenly beings and voices.

Revelation 11 describes the two witnesses on earth, until verse 15 when "the seventh angel sounded [the seventh trumpet]; and there arose loud voices in heaven" praising the Messiah and His Father, as were the twenty-four elders. The chapter ends with verse 19 describing that "the temple of God which is in heaven was opened; and the ark of His covenant appeared in His temple, and there were flashes of lightning and sounds and peals of thunder and an earthquake and a great hailstorm."

Although Revelation 12 begins with "And a great sign appeared in heaven...," the action described in that sign seems to occur on earth when the woman with child is pursued by a great red dragon. Then, there is war in heaven when Michael and his angels throw down to earth the great dragon, Satan, and his angels. After a heavenly message, the chapter ends with more information about the dragon pursuing the woman and "the rest of her offspring" on earth. Since Revelation 13 introduces the two beasts, there is nothing heavenly about it. Their realm is earth.

On the other hand, Revelation 14 is about heaven, until the judgments. In verse 2, John heard "a voice from heaven," followed by the 144,000 singing a new song. Then verse 6 has a second mention of mid-heaven but this time "another angel" is flying there and preaching the eternal gospel. Two more angels give a proclamation and an ultimatum to those on earth. John again hears a voice from heaven, and three more angels appear from heaven to dispense bloody judgment on earth.

Revelation 14 and 15 together are a prelude to the coming final bowl judgments of Revelation 16. Both chapters are set in heaven except the sections of Revelation 14 that reference judgments on earth. In Revelation 15 the seven angels with the seven bowl judgments prepare to dispense them. In heaven there is tremendous praise to the Heavenly Father and the temple fills with smoke. Then, in Revelation 16:1 a loud voice from the temple instructs the seven angels to pour out the seven bowls of His wrath into the earth. While these plagues wreak havoc throughout the entire earth, there is more praise and a blessing from heaven.

Revelation 17 and 18 describe the global political and economic system as well as the worldwide harlot religion on earth. There are references to heaven in that an angel and voices from heaven announce the fall of these two demonic organizations, but they are earthly systems, tools of the antichrist and false prophet.

Revelation 19 takes place in heaven for the most part, as all of heaven praises the Father and rejoices because "the marriage of the Lamb has come and His bride has made herself ready." Then the Messiah rides upon a white horse with His army from heaven, ready for war on earth. Birds in mid-heaven are invited to eat the bodies of the earthly armies killed with the sword of the Messiah, while the antichrist and the false prophet are thrown into the lake of fire, below the earth.

Revelation 20 describes the thousand-year Millennial Kingdom. The events that occur in heaven are the two resurrections and the Great White Throne judgment. The rest takes place on earth or below earth in the abyss.

Revelation 21 portrays a New Heaven and a New Earth. A New Jerusalem comes down out of heaven from the Father. So, the chapter begins in heaven but then describes the earth in its eternal state.

Revelation 22 serves as an epilogue, with references to heaven. Verse 1 mentions the throne of the Heavenly Father from which a river of water of life flows, presumably to the New Earth. Following that are blessings, instructions, warnings and invitations to those on earth.

Chapter 5
Characters of the "Play"

The many "characters" in Revelation can be overwhelming. Some are better known than others. The purpose of going into detail is to become familiar with each one so that distinguishing between them is not a distraction when later tackling more difficult ideas. Some of Revelation's "characters" are awe-inspiring and others are scary, but believers should know all of them. Note the contrast between the well-oiled orchestration of the heavenly creatures and the chaos of the earthly ones.

The book of Revelation is the Father's message concerning His Son, the Messiah. First and foremost, **Yahweh, our Creator and our Heavenly Father,** is described in Revelation 1:4 as "Him who is and who was and who is to come." He expands in verse 8 saying, "I am the Alpha and the Omega,"..."the Almighty." Revelation 4:2-3 describes "One sitting on the throne" in heaven, presumably Yahweh. He is characterized as "like a jasper stone" (clear) "and a sardius" (reddish) in appearance. Revelation 15:7-8 describes Yahweh as "God, who lives forever and ever" just before His power is portrayed as so overwhelming that no one was able to enter the temple in heaven. Revelation 21:5-7 shows "He who sits on the throne" saying "I am the Alpha and the Omega, the beginning and the end. I will give to the one who thirsts from the spring of the water of life without cost. He who overcomes shall inherit these things, and I will be his God and he will be My son."

Almost every other mention of Yahweh in Revelation concerns His Name. Yahweh means "I AM" in Hebrew and is the Name He gave to Moses from the burning bush. Most people know that "His name shall be on [believers'] foreheads."(Rev. 22:4) So, it is critically important to know exactly what His name is, beyond His titles of God and Lord, translations at that. Thankfully, Yahweh is magnanimous enough to love us whatever name we call Him as long as our hearts are pure. But, a day is coming when His name will be crucial. In Revelation 3:8 one of the churches is praised because they "have kept My word, and have not denied My name."

Speaking of His name, Psalm 118:26 says, "Blessed is the one who comes in the name of Yahweh (properly translated)." In fact, the Messiah quotes this verse in Matthew 23:39 when He says, "For I say to you, from now on you shall not see Me until you say, 'Blessed is He who comes in the name of Yahweh!'" This is one of the "when" clues. Pay attention to what all of Scripture says about His Name, including Revelation where there is even mention of His new name (3:12), as well as a name which no one knows except Himself (19:12).

The focus of Revelation is **Messiah, the Worthy Lamb, or the Bridegroom**. The first and fifth chapters are almost exclusively about Him. He is worthy because, as the Slain Lamb, He is the perfect sacrifice for the sins of mankind. Most theories hold that in the future He will come from heaven as a conqueror and judge to be united with His bride, the body of believers.

If examined closely, Revelation gives many descriptions of the Messiah. In Revelation 1:5, He is "the faithful witness, the first-born of the dead, and the ruler of the kings of the earth." He also "loves us and released us from our sins by His blood." Verse 6 goes on to say that "He has made us to be a kingdom, priests to His God and Father." Verse 7 adds, "He is coming with the clouds, and every eye will see Him, even those who pierced Him; and all the tribes of the earth will mourn over Him." Verses 13 through 16 reveal a detailed description of "one like a son of man," obviously the Messiah. He is clothed in a floor length robe with a golden girdle or sash across His breast. With His white hair, flaming eyes, brightly shining face, bronze feet and loud voice, He holds seven stars in His right hand and has a sharp two-edged sword coming out of His mouth. In verses 17 and 18 He refers to Himself as "the first and the last,"… "the living One" who was dead but is now alive forevermore, having the keys of death and Hades.

Interestingly, many of these descriptions are then repeated in the seven letters to the seven churches. In Revelation 2:1 He is the "One who holds the seven stars in His right hand, the One who walks among the seven golden lampstands." Verse 8 says that He is "the first and the last, who was dead, and has come to life." In verse 12 He is "the One who has the sharp two-edged sword." Verse 18 refers to Him as "the Son of God, who has eyes like a flame of fire, and His feet are like burnished bronze." In Revelation 3:1 the Messiah is "He who has the seven Spirits of God, and the seven stars," the latter being the seven angels of the seven churches (Rev. 1:20). In Revelation 3:7 He is described as "He who is holy, who is true, who has the key of David, who opens and no one will shut, and who shuts and no one opens." Verse 14 says that He is "the Amen, the faithful and true Witness, the Beginning of the creation of Yahweh."

Revelation 5:5 refers to Him as the Lion of Judah, the Root of David who "has overcome so as to open the book and its seven seals." In verse 6 He is described as "a Lamb, standing, as if slain, having seven horns and seven eyes, which are the seven Spirits of God," the latter generally considered to be the Holy Spirit. Horns often depict strength. In Revelation 6, the Lamb breaks open the first four seals that release the four horsemen of the apocalypse, as well as the later seals. Then Revelation 7 describes praise in heaven "before the throne and before the Lamb." In verse 10 Yahweh sits on the throne, and verse 17 says that "the Lamb in the center of the throne" is their shepherd who shall guide the tribulation saints "to springs of the water of life; and God shall wipe every tear from their eyes." So, both the Father and the Son are on the throne or thrones together in heaven.

In Revelation 8:1 the Lamb breaks the seventh seal, which unleashes the one-third trumpet judgments. Later on, the only reference to the Lamb in Revelation 12 is verse 11 when, after war in heaven where Michael and his angels throw Satan down to earth, a loud voice in heaven says that the believers overcame Satan "because of the blood of the Lamb." Revelation 13:8 refers to "the book of life of the Lamb who has been slain" in which the names of those who worship Satan have not had their names written "from the foundation of the world."

Then Revelation 14 gives further information about the Lamb. Verse 1 shows the Lamb standing on Mt. Zion with the 144,000 who have "His name and the name of His Father written on their foreheads." These 144,000 are described in verse 4 as "the ones who follow the Lamb wherever He goes," having been "purchased from among man as first fruits to God and the Lamb." In contrast, verse 10 describes unbelievers who receive the mark of the beast as being "tormented with fire and brimstone in the presence of the holy angels and in the presence of the Lamb." In a vision of judgment in verse 14, "one like a son of man" sitting in a white cloud has a golden crown on His head and a sharp sickle in His hand.

Revelation 15:3 refers to the martyrs who "had come off victorious from the beast" singing the song of Moses the bond-servant of Yahweh and the song of the Lamb. Revelation 17:14 says, referring to the "ten horns" of verse 12, that "these will wage war against the Lamb, and the Lamb will overcome them, because He is Lord of lords and King of kings."

Then Revelation 19:7-8 describes the joyful preparations for the marriage feast of the Lamb, while verse 9 proclaims a blessing on "those who are invited to the marriage supper of the Lamb." Verses 11 through 16 reveal the Messiah as a conquering King coming from heaven on a white horse with the armies in heaven clothed in white clean linen also on white horses following Him. In addition to the Messiah's fiery eyes and many diadems upon His Head, He has a sharp sword coming from His mouth and a robe with a name written, "KING OF KINGS AND LORD OF LORDS." He is also called the Word of Yahweh, "Faithful and True." "In righteousness He judges and wages war." "He treads the wine press of the fierce wrath of God, the Almighty." "He will rule them with a rod of iron."

Revelation 21 reveals the Messiah ruling His Millennial Kingdom. Verses 3 and 4 relate that "the tabernacle of God is among men, and He shall dwell among them, and they shall be His people, and God Himself shall be among them, and He shall wipe away every tear from their eyes; and there shall no longer be any death; there shall no longer be any mourning, or crying, or pain." What a magnificent Messiah!

There are many **heavenly creatures**, some of whom are possibly representative of something, such as the twenty-four elders. Then, there are other figures who definitely are representative, such as the "woman with child." A good strategy might be to not worry about this initially, but to consider each as simply a character in a play. What is important is to know them and to be able to distinguish between them by learning details about each one.

Revelation focuses more on **heavenly angels** than satanic ones. The insight gained on heavenly angels in the book of Revelation is phenomenal. There seem to be different kinds, or at the very least they have different roles to play. These heavenly angels praise Yahweh, the Messiah, saints and certain events. In addition, they are given very important jobs to do. More details are given about some than others. As seen throughout the Scriptures, the angels in Revelation are messengers. The Hebrew word for angel also means messenger. They communicate the gospel message, blessings, warnings, orders, invitations and ultimatums. They also seem to control or at least restrain natural forces of the universe. Unlike the typical portrayal of angels as gentle and sweet, some are serious instruments of judgment. A few seem to be particularly strong, or perhaps they are really the Messiah.

In Revelation 1 an angel communicates Yahweh's message of the Messiah's revelation to John. This angel is likely John's guide throughout the entire book. In Revelation 2 and 3, the seven letters are addressed to "the angel of the church in …," presumably different angels for each city. In Revelation 3:5 the Messiah promises to confess he who overcomes, i.e. believers, "before My Father and before His angels." Revelation 5:2 mentions a strong angel who asks with a loud voice, "Who is worthy to open the book and break its seals?"

Revelation 7 is full of angels. First, four angels are "standing at the four corners of the earth, holding back the four winds of the earth." Verse 2b specifies that these are "the four angels to whom it was granted to harm the earth and the sea." Then "another angel ascending from the rising of the sun, having the seal of the living God" cries out with a loud voice to the four other angels not to harm any thing until the bond-servants of our God, the 144,000, have been sealed on their foreheads. Later, in verse 11, all the angels are standing around the throne with other heavenly beings when "they fell on their faces before the throne and worshiped God."

In Revelation 8:3-5 "another angel" holding a golden censer is given much incense at the altar before the throne in order to add it to the prayers of all the saints. When the smoke from the incense goes up before Yahweh, the angel fills the censer with the altar fire and throws it to earth, causing thunder, lightning and an earthquake. This is a prelude to the trumpets. Unlike the seal judgments in Revelation 6 when the Lamb opens each seal, it is angels who sound the trumpets of judgment in Revelation 8 and 9, as well as dispense the bowl judgments in Revelation 16. The question arises as to the significance of this distinction. This is yet another way that the seal judgments are different from the trumpet and bowl judgments.

In Revelation 10:1-7, more description of an angel is given than elsewhere in Revelation. "Another strong angel coming down out of heaven" was clothed with a cloud and had a rainbow upon his head, a face like the sun and feet like pillars of fire. With "a little book" open in his hand, he places his right foot on the sea and his left on the land, and when he cries out as loud as a lion, the seven peals of thunder (angels?) speak but John is instructed not to write it down. Then this strong angel swears with his right hand lifted up to heaven that there would no longer be delay, but "in the days of the voice of the seventh angel, when he is about to sound, then the mystery of

God is finished, as He preached to His servants the prophets." Toward the end of Revelation 11, after the two witnesses, the seventh angel then sounds his trumpet in verse 15, precipitating praise in heaven after an announcement of His coming reign.

Revelation 12:7-9 describes a war in heaven between the dragon, Satan, and his evil angels and the archangel Michael and his angels. The heavenly angels are stronger than the satanic ones who are thrown down to earth. "They were not strong enough, and there was no longer a place found for them in heaven." That's reassuring.

Revelation 14 is part of the prelude prior to the bowl judgments. In verses 6 through 20 six angels perform six different services. First, "another angel flying in mid-heaven" preaches the eternal gospel to every nation and people on earth, probably for the last time because "the hour of His judgment has come." A second angel follows the first one, proclaiming that Babylon the Great has fallen. A third angel issues an ultimatum of fierce judgment for those who worship the beast and receive his mark. A fourth angel "came out of the temple" loudly urging the Messiah to reap judgment. A fifth angel also "came out of the temple which is in heaven," but with a sharp sickle. Then a sixth angel with power over fire "came out from the altar" loudly ordering the fifth angel to reap judgment as well, using the analogy of a wine press. The last verse, quite well-known and often quoted, describes the blood from "the great wine press" to be up to the horses' bridles for a distance of 200 miles.

Revelation 15, with only eight verses, is the second part of the prelude. The seven angels have "seven plagues, which are the last, because in them the wrath of God is finished." After great praise of Yahweh, "the temple of the tabernacle of testimony in heaven was opened and the seven angels who had the seven plagues came out of the temple, clothed in linen, clean and bright, and girded around their breasts with golden girdles." After the four living creatures give them "seven golden bowls full of the wrath of God," the temple fills with smoke from Yahweh's power and glory. "No one was able to enter the temple until the seven plagues of the seven angels were finished."

This scene actually continues in Revelation 16 where the seven angels are instructed to "go pour out the seven bowls of the wrath of God into the earth." As each one does so, worldwide catastrophes devastate the earth. In verses 4 through 6, after the third bowl judgment that causes rivers and springs to turn to blood "the angel of the waters" praises the judgment because it is deserved, "for they poured out the blood of saints and prophets, and Thou hast given them blood to drink."

Then, in Revelation 17 one of the seven angels speaks to John and carries him "away in the Spirit into a wilderness to see the fall of" Babylon the harlot and her scarlet beast, or the fall of the one-world religion and the global government. Revelation 18 begins with "another angel coming down from heaven, having great authority, and the earth was illumined with his glory." This angel announces the fall of Babylon. Later, in verse 18 "a strong angel took up a stone like a great millstone and threw it into the sea," to illustrate the fate of Babylon.

In Revelation 19:1-9, after praise in heaven preparations for the marriage supper are underway when the angel issues a blessing. Then, as a mini-aside in verse 10, John relates his attempt to worship the angel who refers to himself as "a fellow servant of yours and your brethren who hold the testimony of Jesus." After the coming of the Messiah in verses 11 through 16, verse 17 says that John sees "an angel standing in the sun" who invites the "birds which fly in mid-heaven" to eat the flesh of those slaughtered, presumably from the war mentioned in verse 11.

Revelation 20 begins with "an angel coming down from heaven, having the key of the abyss and a great chain in his hand," who binds Satan and throws him into the abyss for 1000 years. How marvelous that His angels are that powerful. Midway through Revelation 21 "one of the seven angels who had the seven bowls full of the seven last plagues" invites John to see the New Jerusalem. Then as part of the epilogue in Revelation 22, an angel reiterates to

John that Yahweh "sent His angel to show to His bond-servants the things which must [quickly] take place." Another mini-aside relates that John tries to worship this angel but is corrected once again not to do so but to worship Yahweh. Then the angel tells John not to seal up the words of Revelation. For the second time in this chapter John is told that an angel was sent to testify to these things for the churches, but this time the Messiah is talking and refers to the angel as "My angel." Counting the same message in Revelation 1:1, this is the third reference to an angel being sent to communicate this prophecy.

Despite the distinct possibility that most of **the voices** in Revelation are probably voices of angels, they will be examined separately because a few at least may be the voice of Yahweh the Father or Messiah the Son or the Holy Spirit. Sometimes the voices are identified but usually they are not. Most seem powerful. Some are a single voice and others are multiple ones. Psalm 29 includes a very descriptive portrayal of the voice of Yahweh as loud and quite powerful. The most common description of the voices in Revelation is also that they are loud, but in addition they are described as sounding like harps as well as many waters, a trumpet and thunder.

In Revelation 1:10-11 John heard behind him "a loud voice like a trumpet" telling him to write in a book what he sees and tell the seven churches. Revelation 4:1, referring to the same voice in Revelation 1, says "the first voice which I had heard, like the sound of a trumpet" invites John to "come up here" to show him what must take place "after these things." Then in Revelation 5:11 John hears "the voice of many angels around the throne" along with the twenty-four elders and four living creatures "saying with a loud voice, 'Worthy is the Lamb that was slain.'" It is obvious to whom these voices belong.

In Revelation 9:13 after the sixth angel sounds his trumpet, John hears "a voice from the four horns of the golden altar which is before God," telling the sixth angel to "release the four angels who are bound at the great river Euphrates." These four angels "who had been prepared for the hour and day and month and year" proceed to kill a third of mankind. It is difficult to consider these to be heavenly angels. What is obvious is that this sixth angel is more powerful than the four angels of death. But it is the voice that initiates the action. This is an instance where the voice very possibly is Yahweh or the Messiah.

Then again in Revelation 10:1-3 the voice is clearly an angel, and this one is described as "a loud voice, as when a lion roars." In the very next verse John hears "a voice from heaven saying, 'Seal up the things which the seven peals of thunder have spoken, and do not write them.'" Verse 7 reveals that "in the days of the voice of the seventh angel, when he is about to sound, then the mystery of God is finished, as He preached to His servants the prophets." In verses 8 and 9, "the voice which I heard from heaven," the one from verse 4, instructs John to take the open little book from the hand of the angel who stands on land and sea, and eat it.

In Revelation 11:12 "a loud voice from heaven" calls the two witnesses to heaven after they have been killed and their bodies have lain in the streets for 3 ½ days. Verse 15 specifies that after the seventh angel sounded his trumpet "there arose loud voices in heaven" praising the Messiah's coming kingdom. After correlating the coming of the Messiah's kingdom with Satan being thrown down out of heaven in Revelation 12:10, "a loud voice in heaven" reveals an important detail about heaven, that Satan accuses believers before Yahweh day and night.

Interestingly, Revelation 14:2 portrays "a voice from heaven" more descriptively than anywhere else. It was "like the sound of many waters and like the sound of loud thunder, and … like the sound of harpists playing on their harps." But there is no mention of what the voice says, unless it is also the voice in verse 13. There, John hears a voice from heaven instructing him to write, "Blessed are the dead who die in the Lord from now on!" The Spirit either chimes in or is the voice. "'Yes,' says the Spirit, 'that they may rest from their labors, for their deeds follow with them.'"

As with the trumpet judgments, the bowl judgments are administered by angels. But unlike the trumpet judgments, the angels pouring out the bowl judgments are directed by "a loud voice from the temple." Were these judgments so horrendous that the angels needed prodding? It's an interesting consideration. Then when the seventh angel finished in Revelation 16:17 "a loud voice came out of the temple from the throne saying, 'It is done.'" Sound familiar?

A fascinating warning in Revelation 18:4-5 is given by "another voice from heaven, saying, 'Come out of her, my people, that you may not receive her plagues, for her sins have piled up as high as heaven, and God has remembered her iniquities.'" "Her" appears to reference Babylon, the harlot religion, to be destroyed in one day. The voice could be the Messiah since it says "my people."

Then in Revelation 19:1 "a loud voice of a great multitude in heaven" praises Yahweh "because His judgments are true and righteous." In verse 5 "a voice came from the throne, saying, 'Give praise to our God, all you His bond-servants, you who fear Him, the small and the great.'" In the next verse John hears "the voice of a great multitude and the sound of many waters and the sound of mighty peals of thunder, saying, 'Hallelujah, for the Lord our God, the Almighty, reigns.'" Lastly, in Revelation 21:3 John hears "a loud voice from the throne, saying, 'Behold, the tabernacle of God is among men, and He shall dwell among them, and they shall be His people, and God Himself shall be among them, and He shall wipe away every tear from their eyes; and there shall no longer be any death; there shall no longer be any mourning, or crying, or pain, the first things have passed away.'"

The **twenty-four elders and four living creatures** are heavenly beings, maybe representative of specific persons or groups, and maybe not. Matthew 19:28 and Luke 22:30 say that the twelve disciples will sit on twelve thrones to judge the twelve tribes. So if they are twelve of these twenty-four elders, who are the other twelve? Patriarchs and/or prophets? Some scholars view them as angels. Not surprisingly, many theories have been thrown out there as to who they are or what they represent. It's just possible that this will be one of those mysteries revealed upon arrival to heaven. Most of the time, both of these groups are seen together, working in concert with one another, but occasionally they are separate and distinct. Usually, they are worshiping Yahweh or the Messiah with words of praise or with song.

Both the twenty-four elders and the four living creatures are introduced in Revelation 4. The twenty-four elders are sitting on twenty-four thrones which surround *the* throne in heaven. The twenty-four elders are clothed in white garments and have crowns on their heads (vs. 4). Verses 10 and 11 describe their worship of Yahweh as "falling down before Him who sits on the throne" and casting their crowns before the throne. This is described again in Revelation 11:16, but with an added detail. "And the twenty-four elders who sit on their throne before God fell on their faces and worshiped God, saying, 'We give Thee thanks, O Lord God, the Almighty, who art and who wast, because Thou hast taken Thy great power and hast begun to reign.'"

In Revelation 5:5 one of the elders says to John, "Stop weeping, behold the Lion that is from the tribe of Judah, the Root of David, has overcome so as to open the book and the seven seals." Revelation 7:13-14 relates that one of the elders interacts with John about the identity of the tribulation saints in an interesting question and answer exchange.

Even more fascinating than the elders are the four living creatures. Revelation 4:6-9 describes them as "full of eyes in front and behind" or "around and within," depending on the translation. Each one has six wings. "They do not cease to say, 'Holy, holy, holy is the Lord God, the Almighty, who was and who is and who is to come.'" So, are they angels or maybe archangels? One theologian proposes that they are because Isaiah 6:2-3 says that seraphim surround Yahweh's throne in heaven, as do the four living creatures. But, what excludes the possibility that both groups are there?

Unlike the twenty-four elders each of the four living creatures is described as being very distinct, but note the use of the word "like." The first creature has a face like a lion, the second creature like that of a calf, the third creature like that of a man and the fourth creature like a flying eagle. In Revelation 6, as the seals are broken by the Lamb, each living creature commands one of the four horsemen of the apocalypse to "come." In Revelation 15:7 "one of the four living creatures gave to the seven angels seven golden bowls full of the wrath of God, who lives forever and ever." But there is no mention of their involvement in the earlier one-third trumpet judgments.

In Revelation 4:9-10 the cooperation between the twenty-four elders and the four living creatures becomes apparent. "And when the living creatures give glory…to Him…, the twenty-four elders will fall down… and worship Him." More details are seen in Revelation 5. Verse 8 states that "when He had taken the book, the four living creatures and twenty-four elders fell down before the Lamb, having each one a harp and golden bowls full of incense, which are the prayers of the saints." Then they sing a new song praising the Messiah. Verse 14, again showing cooperation and coordination, says that the four living creatures keep saying "Amen" and the elders fall down and worship. Revelation 7:11 elaborates, in that "all the angels were standing around the throne and around the elders and the four living creatures; and they fell on their faces before the throne and worshiped God." Revelation 19:4 demonstrates the same praise and worship. And yet, a new song is sung "before the throne and before the four living creatures and the elders, and no one could learn the song except the 144,000. (Rev. 14:3).

Revelation 7 introduces **the 144,000**, about whom there is a fair amount of controversy. Their identity is the focus of much attention since they are obviously important, but the details are somewhat nebulous and indeterminate. Even their location is in question. While Revelation 7 appears to take place on earth, Revelation 14 is less clear but seems to indicate that they are in heaven.

In Revelation 7:1-3, "four angels standing at the four corners of the earth, holding back the four winds of the earth," are directed by "another angel ascending from the rising of the sun" not to harm the earth or the sea or the trees until they have sealed the bond-servants of our God on their foreheads. The next verse then introduces the 144,000 as being "from every tribe of the sons of Israel." Verses 5 through 8 explain that there are 12,000 from each of the twelve tribes. The list of the names of the twelve tribes is not exactly the same as the list of the twelve sons of Jacob in Genesis nor is that list consistent throughout the Bible, but this doesn't interfere with learning the basics. Then the subject abruptly changes in verse 9 when "after these things" John saw a great multitude in heaven, seemingly distinct from the 144,000.

The 144,000 are not seen again until Revelation 14:1-5, when they are standing on Mt. Zion (presumably Jerusalem) with the Lamb. They have His name and the name of His Father written on their foreheads. They are blameless, in that they do not lie; they are chaste, or have not been defiled with women; they follow the Lamb wherever He goes; and they have been "purchased from among men as first fruits to God and to the Lamb." This and the fact that they have been "purchased from the earth" indicate that they are at some point in heaven. As stated, "they sang a new song before the throne and before the four living creatures and the elders and no one could learn the song," except the 144,000. This group is definitely exceptional, and is so in several ways.

The proposals put forward on the identity of the 144,000 range from their being Hebrew evangelists to simply being representative of Hebrew believers. One source posits that they are the Messiah's groomsmen for the upcoming wedding (Klein/Spears). Some question whether they are specific patriarchs from ancient history or whether they are representatives of all Hebrew patriarchs. Revelation 7:3 calls them bond-servants of Yahweh and Revelation 15:3 refers to Moses as the bond-servant of Yahweh, as is John (Rev. 1:1). Revelation 11:18 seems to distinguish between "Thy bond-servants the prophets and ... the saints," but also mentions "those who fear Thy name." So, are they distinct or all one and the same?

Bond-servants are mentioned throughout Scripture, including Revelation. Revelation 22:3 says that "His bond-servants shall serve Him" in the New Kingdom; "they shall see His face, and His name shall be on their foreheads." Revelation 22:6 says that His angel was sent "to show His bond-servants the things which must shortly take place," a repetition of its use in Revelation 1:1. To help simplify the matter, consider bond-servants to at least be believers and keep an open mind about the 144,000.

Throughout Revelation **martyrs and tribulation saints** are mentioned. They are likely recent ones, added to the numbers of saints and martyrs down through the ages who are already in heaven. Of course they are believers or brethren, also bond-servants, but both of these groups are special in that they are singled out in a noticeable way. Martyrs are considered to be those who have died for their beliefs. The tribulation saints, believers during the tribulation, presumably have not been martyred.

The martyrs are introduced after the fifth seal is broken in Revelation 6:9 as the "souls of those who had been slain because of the word of God and because of the testimony which they had maintained." Verse 11 indicates that they are anxious for justice, loudly crying out, asking how long until judgment. The response is "that they should rest for a little while longer, until the number of their fellow servants and their brethren who were to be killed even as they had been, should be completed also."

In Revelation 12:11, possibly alluding to those very martyrs who were yet to be killed, "they overcame [Satan] because of the blood of the Lamb and because of the word of their testimony, and they did not love their life even to death." In Revelation 19:2b, likely referring to all martyrs, "He has avenged the blood of His bond-servants on [the harlot Babylon]." Then, Revelation 20:4-6 refers specifically to the later martyrs "beheaded because of the testimony of Jesus and because of the word of God," but also mentions those who did not receive the mark of the beast, likely the tribulation saints. Both groups "came to life and reigned with Christ for a thousand years" as a part of the first resurrection, while "the rest of the dead did not come to life until the thousand years were completed."

In Revelation 7:9 the tribulation saints are described as "a great multitude, which no one could count, from every nation..., standing before the throne and before the Lamb, clothed in white robes, and palm branches were in their hands." Verses 13 and 14 show that after one of the elders asks who they are and John replies that the elder knows, this same elder acknowledges that they are "the ones who come out of the great tribulation and they have washed their robes and made them white in the blood of the Lamb." In verse 15 "they serve Him day and night in His temple; and He who sits on the throne shall spread His tabernacle over them." As verses 16 and 17 depict, they will suffer no more from heat, thirst, hunger or sadness. The Lamb "shall be their shepherd, and shall guide them to springs of the water of life." There is no hint of execution, though there seems to have been persecution.

If Revelation 15:2 is referring to the tribulation saints, "those who had come off victorious from the beast and from his image and from the number of his name," then they likely survive at least a portion of the tribulation period. To "come off victorious," not to mention "come out of," can be interpreted in various ways. It could indicate believers who survive the tribulation and then are raptured or it could point to saints who are in fact martyred at some point during the tribulation.

Several times saints are mentioned that are not specifically tribulation saints. Also, not every mention of a great multitude is necessarily tribulation saints. In Revelation 19:1 "a loud voice of a great multitude in heaven" praising Yahweh, also repeated in verse 6, may be the tribulation saints but it could also include all heavenly beings. It just is not clear. The best course may be to keep an open mind on the specific identity of not only these two groups but the next two personalities as well.

Revelation 11 introduces **the two witnesses**, more well-known in Christian circles than most of the other "characters." Despite a brief twelve verses about them, they are the center of much attention and much speculation. The majority of theologians believe them to be Moses and Elijah, but there is no definitive proof in the Bible. Since their appearance will be unmistakable when it happens, their exact identity is not necessary to know ahead of time. As Corrie ten Boom's father liked to explain, our Heavenly Father will give His children the necessary ticket for the train just before it arrives. Why would they need it sooner?

Though an end time event, the exact timing of the appearance of the two witnesses is also not entirely clear. Verses 1 and 2 may indicate that they operate after the third temple is built. Verses 3 through 6 give details of their earthly ministry. "The two olive trees and the two lampstands that stand before the Lord of the earth," clothed in sackcloth will be granted authority by Yahweh to prophesy for 1260 days (41 months or 3 ½ years) with great powers to kill their enemies by fire from their mouths, to stop the rain, to turn water to blood and to "smite the earth with every plague, as often as they desire." Because of the 3 ½-year length, the logical assumption is that they will appear during either the first or second half of the seven-year tribulation period.

Their death and resurrection are described in verses 7 through 12. "And when they have finished their testimony, the beast that comes up out of the abyss will make war with them," and kill them. For 3 ½ days "their dead bodies will lie in the street," of Jerusalem most agree, while the world sees this and rejoices. People will send gifts to one another "because these two prophets tormented those who dwell on the earth." After 3 ½ days "the breath of life from God came into them, and they stood on their feet; and great fear fell upon those who were beholding them." They go up into heaven in the cloud, as "their enemies beheld them." And in that exact hour, there is a great earthquake, destroying one-tenth of the city, killing 7000 people and terrifying the rest to the point that they "gave glory to the God of heaven." (vs.13)

The "woman" of Revelation 12:1-6 is mentioned only in that chapter. Both the woman and her adversary, the dragon, are referred to as "a sign [which] appeared in heaven." The woman is generally believed to represent Israel. She is "clothed with the sun and the moon under her feet and on her head a crown of twelve stars; and she was with child." The dragon or Satan "stood before [her], ... so that when she gave birth he might devour her child." She gives birth to a son, the Messiah, a male child who is caught up to Yahweh and His throne. "And the woman fled into the wilderness where she had a place prepared by God, so that there she might be nourished 1260 days (3 ½ years)." This might be referring to Mary and Joseph's flight to Egypt or to over two thousand years later during the tribulation, or both, thus having a double meaning.

There is war in heaven (vs. 7-9) with Michael and his angels prevailing over the dragon Satan and his angels. The indication in verses 10 and 11 is that this occurs as a result of the Messiah's crucifixion. "For the accuser of our brethren has been thrown down... and they overcame him because of the blood of the Lamb." And of course, the heavenly angels were stronger that the satanic ones, as mentioned.

Then verses 13 through 17 explain that "when the dragon saw that he was thrown down to the earth, he persecuted the woman (Israel)... And the two wings of the great eagle were given to the woman, in order that she might fly into the wilderness to her place, where she was nourished for a time and times and half a time (usually interpreted to be 3 ½ years of the tribulation) from the presence of the serpent. And the serpent poured water like a river out of his mouth after the woman, so that he might cause her to be swept away with the flood. And the earth helped the woman, and the earth opened its mouth and drank up the river which the dragon poured out of his mouth." Enraged, the dragon "went off to make war with the rest of her offspring who keep the commandments of God and hold to the testimony of Jesus." Interpretations abound and it is particularly important to be very judicious with sections so mysterious.

The "Bride" is mentioned in Revelation 19 and 21. In Revelation 19:7-8 "the marriage of the Lamb has come and His bride has made herself ready. And it was given to her to clothe herself in fine linen, bright and clean; for the fine linen is the righteous acts of the saints." So here she clearly is the body of believers.

In Revelation 21:2 John "saw the holy city, new Jerusalem, coming down out of heaven from God, made ready as a bride adorned for her husband." Note the word "as." Then in verses 9 and 10 one of the seven angels who had the seven bowls spoke with John, saying "Come here, I shall show you the bride, the wife of the Lamb. And he carried me away in the Spirit to a great and high mountain and showed me the holy city, Jerusalem, coming down out of heaven from Yahweh." There is no use of "like" or "as" here. Verses 11 through 27 describe the city in detail. Then verse 27b explains that in it are "only those whose names are written in the Lamb's book of life," believers.

Although there is disagreement as to whether **John** the writer of Revelation is the apostle John, he is described as "His bond-servant, ... who bore witness to the word of God and to the testimony of Jesus Christ, even to all that he saw." In Revelation 1 John introduces himself as "your brother and fellow partaker in the tribulation and kingdom and perseverance which are in Jesus." Note that tribulation here is used for persecution that is not in the end of days. He says his location at the time of the writing is Patmos. He goes on the say that he "was in the Spirit on the Lord's day." "A loud voice like the sound of a trumpet" instructs John to write what he sees and send it to the seven churches named. He beholds the glorified Messiah, which causes him to fall down "as a dead man." He is told not to fear, and is again instructed to write what he has seen.

In Revelation 4, John sees "a door standing open in heaven" and is invited to "come up here" to see "what must take place." Immediately he is "in the Spirit" and beholds the splendor of heaven's throne room and all its occupants. In Revelation 5, upon seeing a sealed book John weeps greatly until the worthy Lamb opens it. Thereafter, John views events in heaven and on earth: a series of judgments dispensed, visions of the 144,000 and the multitude of tribulation saints, angels on specific missions, two witnesses with great powers, a woman pursued by a dragon, war in heaven, the beast and the false prophet, the harlot one-world religion and the beastly global government of the devilish duo, the Messiah's marriage preparations and His second coming, the Millennial Kingdom and the New Heaven and New Earth.

Twice John is "carried away," once in Revelation 17:3 to a wilderness to see the harlot Babylon and again in Revelation 21:10 to "a great and high mountain" to see the New Jerusalem. What a contrast! Throughout the entire book of Revelation, John is puzzled and likely frightened, but he is always awed, even to the point of falling down to worship an angel twice and the glorified Messiah once.

Last but unfortunately not least, an **evil trio** operates as a counterfeit imitation of the blessed Trinity created by Yahweh. Satan's two stooges are the antichrist and the false prophet. Many see the former as a worldwide political leader and the latter as a religious leader. For the sake of simplicity, that theory will help distinguish between them. Throughout the Scriptures, there is mention of Satan or the devil, but only in Revelation is there a good picture of his two minions.

According to Revelation 20:2, **Satan** is the devil, the serpent of old as well as the dragon of the end times. Revelation 9:1 describes

Satan as "a star from heaven which had fallen to earth; and the key of the bottomless pit was given to him." Revelation 12:3-4 reveals Satan as "a great red dragon having seven heads and ten horns, and on his head were seven diadems. And his tail swept away a third of the stars of heaven, and threw them to earth." These descriptions can be interpreted multiple ways. For now it's only important to be familiar with the information. Also note that at times the word serpent is used interchangeably with dragon.

Revelation 2:13 indicates that the earth is "where Satan's throne is" and "where Satan dwells." Revelation 12:7-12 describes Satan and his angels being thrown down to earth after his battle with Michael and his angels, in order that Satan no longer might accuse the brethren before Yahweh night and day. So, it sounds like Satan could come and go from earth to heaven before the battle with Michael but his domain has always been earth. It is hard to know where this heavenly battle fits with earth's chronology of other events, if it even can be correlated. After Satan is thrown out of heaven because thankfully his angels "were not strong enough" (vs. 8-9) against Michael and his angels, some see him becoming desperate to derail Yahweh's plans for the future.

Verse 4 mentions that Satan the dragon threatens the "woman with child" but he is thwarted "because of the blood of the Lamb and because of the word of their testimony, and they did not love their life even to death." (vs. 11) "Their" and "they" seem to refer either to the brethren or the martyrs, or maybe both. Verse 12 explains that "the devil has come down to [earth], having great wrath, knowing that he has only a short time." If Satan was thrown down at Messiah's crucifixion, he has had two thousand years. "When the dragon saw that he was thrown down to the earth, he persecuted the woman who gave birth to the male child." (vs.13) Israel and the Jews *have* been continuously and severely persecuted over the last two millennia.

In verse 14 the woman escapes the dragon when she is flown on the two wings of the great eagle into the wilderness "to her place" for 3 ½ years. Verses 15 through 16 recount the serpent's pursuit of her (Israel) with flood water, whether literal or symbolic. When that fails "the dragon was enraged with the woman, and went off to make war with the rest of her offspring, who keep the commandments of God and hold to the testimony of Jesus." (vs.17) Since Adam, Satan has always made it a point to go after believers, so it's unclear where any of this also fits chronologically. Many see it as the tribulation, but there could always be multiple meanings.

One thing is certain, though. In Revelation 20 Satan is bound for a thousand years, during the Millennium, before being released in order to deceive the nations and gather them for a last war. The immense armies under his sway surround Jerusalem but are devoured by fire from heaven. Then Satan is "thrown into the lake of fire and brimstone, where the beast and the false prophet are also; and they shall be tormented day and night forever and ever." Hallelujah!

Revelation 13 lays out the basic facts on **the antichrist and the false prophet**. They are described as two different beasts. The first one came "up out of the sea, having ten horns and seven heads, and on his horns were ten diadems; and on his heads were blasphemous names." This is similar to Satan's description in Revelation 12. The first beast is like a leopard but with bear feet and a lion's mouth. His power, throne and great authority are from the dragon, Satan. John sees "one of his heads as if it had been slain," and his "fatal" wound was healed, amazing the whole earth who then follow him and worship him, as well as the dragon. Fatal is in italics because it may be a fake, since it was "as if it had been slain." Verses 14 and 15 describe another fake, an image of the beast that is given breath and speech, a feat definitely possible with today's technology. Amidst all this he blasphemes Yahweh and His Name and His tabernacle for the forty-two months, or 3 ½ years, that he is given authority over every tribe and nation. Most agree that this is the antichrist.

Interestingly, before the other beast is introduced two urgent warnings are given. Verse 9 exhorts, "If anyone has an ear, let him hear." The next verse reminds everyone of a well-known scriptural principle, that there is no escaping the justice of judgment.

Halfway through Revelation 13 a second beast is introduced, this one "coming up out of the earth," not the sea. It is described as having "two horns like a lamb" but "he spoke as a dragon." Matthew 7:15 similarly depicts false prophets as ravenous wolves in sheep's clothing. They are not what they appear to be. This second beast forces all who dwell on earth to worship the first beast, deceiving everyone by performing great signs and causing all men to be given the mark of 666 on their right hand or on their forehead in order to buy and sell. Revelation 19:20 says that he "performed the signs in [antichrist's] presence, by which he deceived those who had received the mark of the beast and those who worshiped his image." This is generally considered to be the false prophet.

In Revelation 16, between the sixth and seventh bowl judgments, John sees "three unclean spirits like frogs,...spirits of demons, performing signs." One is from the mouth of the dragon Satan, one is from the mouth of the beast or antichrist and one is from the mouth of the false prophet. It is not clear why they are described as being *like* frogs. Verse 14 indicates that their purpose is to gather the kings of the earth "for the war of the great day of God." "And they gathered them together to the place which in Hebrew is called Har-Magedon."(vs. 16) The armies gather there, so presumably they fight there as well. This precedes the ever-so-devastating final bowl judgment, and is a thousand years before the war against Jerusalem in Revelation 20.

These two diabolical characters are connected in Revelation 17 and 18 with the city Babylon, likely the headquarters for the false prophet's harlot religion (Rev. 17:18), and possibly also the antichrist's one-world government. Despite different theories on all of this it may help to view these characters in this way for now.

Revelation 17:1-6 describes a harlot religion that "sits on many waters," and verse 15 explains that "the waters …are peoples and multitudes and nations and tongues." The kings of the earth commit acts of immorality with her and everyone buys into her immorality, likely a one-world religion, a let's-all-worship-the-same-god (probably the antichrist) type. Some claim it is the Catholic Church but are the other denominations so innocent? No way!

John sees a vision of the harlot sitting on a scarlet beast which is likely the antichrist. Maybe the religion is carried, as in supported financially and legally, by the one-world government although "she reigns over the kings of the earth." Revelation 17:4-5 says that the name written on her forehead, a mystery, is "BABYLON THE GREAT, THE MOTHER OF HARLOTS AND OF THE ABOMINATIONS OF THE EARTH." This religion is evidently responsible for killing many believers (martyrs). Verse 6 indicates that John was puzzled at the fact that "the woman was drunk with the blood of the saints." Several descriptions indicate that the religion is wealthy as well as powerful, but at some point the beast and his earthly "ten horns" destroy the harlot religion. Now that's justice.

The focus on the antichrist beast in Revelation 17:8-14 seems to be an explanation for John. The problem is that it sounds more like a riddle. What may help is to consider it to be an imitation of the description of Yahweh, Who is, Who was and Who is to come. "The beast that you saw was and is not, and is about to come up out of the abyss and to go to destruction. And those who dwell on the earth will wonder, [unbelievers], when they see the beast, that he was and is not and will come." Three verses later it continues with, "And the beast which was and is not, is himself also an eighth, and is one of the seven, and he goes to destruction." The "eighth" may be a reference to Daniel's eighth beast kingdom. The "seven" is likely referring to the seven heads of the beast, but what that seven may represent is not obvious. In another explanation that turns out to be unclear, verse 9 states, "Here is the mind which has wisdom. The seven heads are seven mountains on which the woman sits, and they are seven kings; five have fallen, one is, the other has not yet come; and when he comes, he must remain a little while." This too appears to relate to information in the book of Daniel. When theories propose modern

Katie Snyder

Rome as Babylon it helps to remember that Rome is not the only city with seven hills.

Revelation 17:18 reveals that "the woman whom [John] saw is the great city, which reigns over the kings of the earth." So the harlot religion is clearly connected with the city. Immediately following, Revelation 18:2-9 seems to be a description of the fall of Babylon, the universal religion with its headquarters in a city named Babylon, whether a literal or symbolic name. Believers are warned to "come out of her," since her plagues (pestilence, mourning, famine and fire) will come in one day and will be "double according to her deeds." Her judgment comes in one hour! Then verses 10 through 24 seem to describe an economic and political system, most likely the one-world government of the antichrist. "The merchants of the earth weep and mourn over her."(vs. 11) All luxuries will be no longer available. There will be no music, no work, no light and no joy, all because she deceived the nations and killed the saints.

After the marriage feast of Revelation 19:7-9, verses 11 through 19 abruptly change to show "the beast and the kings of the earth and their armies assembled to make war against [Messiah]," and His army from heaven. The beast, or antichrist, is seized with the false prophet and they are thrown alive into the lake of fire, while the rest who came to make war are killed by Messiah's sword. Satan is then bound for 1000 years during the Millennial Kingdom and later he too is thrown into the lake of fire.

In addition to the evil trio, Revelation mentions **other beings** which one might assume are satanic but it just is not entirely clear. Yahweh is known for using evil persons for His purposes. These "characters" are both human and animal.

In Revelation 6 the four horsemen of the Apocalypse are on white, red, black and gray horses. In Revelation 9:13-19 "armies of horsemen" 200 million strong have riders with "breastplates the color of fire and of hyacinth and of brimstone, and the heads of the horses are like the heads of lions, and out of their mouths proceed fire and smoke and brimstone." Note the word "like." A third of mankind is killed by this weapon from their mouths after the sixth trumpet precipitates the release of the four angels bound at the Euphrates River who had been prepared for this very time.

Also, in Revelation 9:1-12, as a result of the fifth trumpet judgment, "locusts came forth upon the earth from the bottomless pit" to torment unbelievers for five months with a scorpion-like sting that will cause people to want to die. Note the use of the words "like" and "as" here as well. These locusts appear as "horses prepared for battle," maybe armored; "and on their heads, as it were, crowns like gold, and their faces were like the faces of men. And they had hair like women" and teeth like lions. Their breastplates are like iron, their wings sound like chariots, their tails sting like scorpions, and their king is the angel of the abyss named Abaddon or "destruction." John is describing a fantastical sight the best he can, whether they are heavily armed helicopters as some have suggested or they are actual beings.

The **birds** mentioned in Revelation should not be overlooked but they don't fit into the same category as the other animals just mentioned. Their purpose seems positive, some more obviously than others. In Revelation 8:13 "an eagle flying in mid-heaven" announces, "Woe, woe, woe to those who dwell on the earth because of the remaining blasts of the trumpet of the three angels who are about to sound!" In Revelation 19:17-19 "birds which fly in mid-heaven" are invited to feast on the flesh of men and horses that have "assembled to make war against [Messiah]."

Revelation 12:14 says that "the two wings of the great eagle" were given to the woman with child clothed with the sun and a crown of stars (Israel) "in order that she might fly into the wilderness." Is it an actual eagle or a plane with an eagle emblem on it? One must always keep in mind that John used what he knew of his life experience 2000 years ago to describe things difficult for him to process.   At the same time, he was quite familiar with Old Testament usage of the image of eagles' wings providing rescue.

Chapter 6
Props and Costumes for the "Play"

Props and costumes seem to play an integral role in Revelation, as they do in most plays. This is evidenced simply by their inclusion in Revelation. It's easy to make too much of minor things but since there is potential value in understanding certain items and articles of clothing it makes sense to take a close though brief look at them.

As far as **props** are concerned, several different types of books are mentioned throughout Revelation. The most obvious is the scroll with the seven seals in Revelation 5:1-8. John saw it "in the right hand of Him who sat on the throne ..., written inside and on the back, sealed up with seven seals." Is it important that words are written on both sides? Interestingly, the Ten Commandments are. A strong angel asks who is worthy "to open the book and break its seal?" No one was "able to open the book, or to look into it," except the Lamb, the Lion of Judah. The Messiah "took it out of the right hand of Him who sat on the throne." When He took the book, the twenty-four elders and four living creatures fell down before the Lamb." This very important book or scroll unleashes judgment.

Another book, this one in Revelation 10, is the "little book, which was open" in the hand of "another strong angel coming down out of heaven, clothed with a cloud; and the rainbow was upon his head, and his face was like the sun, and his feet like pillars of fire." After he cries out "with a loud voice, as when a lion roars," the seven peals of thunder utter their voices. John is about to write when he hears a voice from heaven tell him to "seal up the things which the seven peals of thunder have spoke, and do not write them." Further along in Revelation 10 the angel instructs John to take the book and eat it. The little book is sweet in his mouth but bitter in his stomach, as the angel had forewarned him. Theories abound for all this as well.

Impossible to underestimate its importance, the book of life is mentioned in several chapters of Revelation. "He who overcomes shall thus be clothed in white garments; and I will not erase his name from the book of life, and I will confess his name before My Father and before His angels." (Rev. 3:5) "And all who dwell on the earth will worship [the dragon], everyone whose name has not been written from the foundation of the world in the book of life of the Lamb who has been slain." (Rev. 13:8) In just these two verses, questions arise concerning eternal destiny and predestination, a theological subject which cannot be addressed here.

Referring to the New Jerusalem, "nothing unclean and no one who practices abomination and lying shall ever come into it, but only those whose names are written in the Lamb's book of life." (Rev. 21:27) "And I saw the dead, the great and small, standing before the throne, and books were opened; and another book was opened, which is the book of life; and the dead were judged from the things which were written in the books, according to their deeds." (Rev. 20:18) So, it seems like there is one book of life and multiple books with everyone's deeds recorded. Maybe the most important thing to remember is that "if anyone's name was not found written in the book of life, he was thrown into the lake of fire." (Rev. 20:15)

Not only is there a book of life, but there is also a tree of life and a crown of life, as well as the breath of life that resurrected the two witnesses. In Revelation 2:7 the letter to Ephesus ends with "…to him who overcomes I will grant to eat of the tree of life, which is in the Paradise of God." The next letter, to Smyrna, includes a promise in verse 10. "Be faithful until death, and I will give you the crown of life." Revelation 22 has two references to the tree of life. In verse 14, "Blessed are those who wash their robes, that they may have the right to the tree of life, and may enter by the gates into the city." Then a warning in verses 18 and 19 says that John testifies to all who hear this prophecy that if anyone takes away from the words of this prophecy, "God shall take away his part from the tree of life and from the holy city, which are written in this book."

Other than nouns used in descriptions, especially comparisons or analogies, the remaining items or objects mentioned in Revelation either do not have much information about them or they are self-exclamatory. There are the obvious trumpets and bowls (some of incense and some of wrath), but also harps, an altar, incense, a measuring rod, a temple and a tabernacle. In relation to judgment are a sickle, a sharp two-edged sword, a great sword, a bow, a pair of scales, a wine press and the key and chain to the abyss. Natural items can be found, such as water, rivers, mountains, a stone, clouds and stars, palm branches and more. How important are they? It's hard to know. It may suffice to just be aware of them.

Details on **clothing, or costumes,** appear throughout Revelation, for both heavenly beings and earthly ones. Presumably the clothing is important simply because these specifics are mentioned. The challenge is in determining how important it is, deciding whether something is symbolic and if so, figuring out what it may symbolize. Don't forget that any theories are just that – theories.

In Revelation 1:13 "one like a Son of Man, clothed in a robe reaching to the feet, and girded across His breast with a golden girdle," has white hair, flaming eyes, feet like hot bronze and "His voice was like the sound of many waters." In Revelation 4:4 the twenty-four elders are "clothed in white garments and golden crowns."

Revelation 3:18 advises believers to clothe themselves with white garments purchased from Him, "that the shame of [their] nakedness may not be revealed." They are His righteous covering for our sinful nature. White is generally believed to represent purity. Revelation 6:11 (fifth seal) says, "And there was given to each [martyr] a white robe." In Revelation 7:9 a great multitude "from every nation and all tribes and peoples and tongues" are clothed in white robes. Then in verses 13 and 14 one of the elders asks John who these people are dressed in white robes, but he answers his own question saying, "These are the ones who come out of the great tribulation, and they have washed their robes and made them white in the blood of the Lamb." Revelation 16:15 says, "Blessed is the one who stays awake and keeps his garment, lest he walk about naked and men see his shame." This may be related to Revelation 3:18 above.

Note that the two witnesses in Revelation 11:3 are described as being "clothed in sackcloth," a sign of mourning or repentance. Almost definitely symbolic, the woman in Revelation 12 is "clothed with the sun and the moon under her feet, and on her head a crown of twelve stars." She is generally regarded to be Israel, since she gives birth to a child that is pursued by Satan, and that child is "caught up to God and His throne." So the twelve stars probably represent the twelve tribes of Israel. The rest is uncertain. In Revelation 15:6 "the seven angels who had the seven plagues came out of the temple, clothed in linen, clean and bright, and girded around their breasts with golden girdles." These girdles are likely wide sashes or belts around the waist area.

Even some of the evil characters are described in detail. In Revelation 17 and 18 the great harlot of Babylon is "clothed in purple and scarlet and adorned with gold and precious stones and pearls." The assumption is that this symbolizes wealth. A few verses later an evil alliance "will hate the harlot and will make her desolate and naked" as part of her destruction. Revelation 18:16 repeats the same description of her clothing, with the detail of linen added.

Linen is significantly mentioned several times. Revelation 19:8 says, "And it was given to [the Bride] to clothe herself in fine linen, bright and clean, for the fine linen is the righteous acts of the saints." In verse 13 the Messiah "is clothed with a robe dipped in blood," while in verse 14 following behind Him are "the armies which are in heaven clothed in fine linen, white and clean." But linen is not mentioned in the last blessing, "Blessed are those who wash their robes, that they may have the right to the tree of life, and may enter by the gates into the city." (Rev. 22:14)

Crowns seem to be a prominent part of clothing for some. As mentioned already Revelation 2:10 refers to a crown of life given to those "faithful until death." Revelation 3:11 advises, "I am coming quickly; hold fast what you have, in order that no one take your crown." This is sandwiched between two very important promises.

The twenty-four elders introduced in Revelation 4:4 who are clothed in white have crowns on their heads. In verse 10 they "cast their crowns before the throne" as they fall down to worship "Him who sits on the throne." The woman with child in Revelation 12:1 is "clothed with the sun, and the moon under her feet, and on her head a crown of twelve stars." Revelation 14:14 describes "One like a son of man having a golden crown on His head." So, crowns are on the Messiah, believers, heavenly creatures, and the woman representing Israel. But they are also seen on one of the infamous horsemen, the mysterious locusts and the first satanic beast.

In Revelation 6:2 a crown was given to the first horseman of the apocalypse, "he who sat on" the white horse with bow in hand as "he went out conquering and to conquer." Revelation 9:7 describes the locusts as having "on their heads, as it were, crowns like gold." They have something on their heads that resembles crowns which are gold, at least in color anyway. Then in Revelation 13:1 "a beast coming up out of the sea having ten horns and seven heads, and on his horns were ten diadems, and on his heads were blasphemous names." A diadem is defined by Webster as a headband worn as a badge of royalty, so it is similar to a crown. There are definitely different kinds of crowns – another mystery.

Chapter 7
Blessings, Promises and Praise

Though unrelated to a play, certain things mentioned in Revelation may be understood better if grouped together and examined. With the inordinate amount of details in Revelation it is easy to read right over parts that seem more familiar, such as blessings, promises and praise. Yet, these may be at least as important as the many puzzling and unfamiliar details. It's worth a look.

The **blessings** concern eternal destiny. Two of them exhort heeding the words of prophecy, and in a related theme, one admonishes staying awake, that is, keeping alert. The remaining four encourage believers to wash their robes, get invited to the marriage supper of the Lamb, die in Yahweh and have a part in the first resurrection. There are seven blessings – the perfect number! A few considerations might include why they are in that particular order, what their connection might be to each other and to other parts of Revelation, and whether all together they paint a picture.

Revelation 1:3 says, "Blessed is he who reads and those who hear the words of the prophecy, and heed the things which are written in it; for the time is [quick]." Revelation 22:7 repeats the same idea, so it must be important. "And behold, I am coming quickly. Blessed is he who heeds the words of the prophecy of this book." Then Revelation 14:13 says, "Blessed are the dead who die in the Lord from now on! 'Yes,' says the Spirit, 'that they may rest from their labors, for their deeds follow with them.'"

Before the blessing in Revelation 16:15 the Messiah warns, "Behold, I am coming like a thief." This applies only to unbelievers (Rev. 3:3). "Blessed is the one who stays awake and keeps his garments, lest he walk about naked and men see his shame." Revelation 19:9 proclaims, "Blessed are those who are invited to the marriage supper of the Lamb." And it is important to be ready for this event, as the Messiah advises in His parable of the ten virgins going out to meet the bridegroom. Matthew 25:1-13 ends with, "Be on the alert then, for you do not know the day nor the hour." Additionally, this particular blessing is followed with, "These are true words of God."

In Revelation 20:6, "Blessed and holy is the one who has a part in the first resurrection; over these the second death has no power, but they will be priests of God and of Christ and will reign with Him for 1000 years." Revelation 22:14 specifies, "Blessed are those who wash their robes, that they may have the right to the tree of life, and may enter by the gates into the city." Whether or not a progression, or any kind of connection, is uncovered believers should pay close attention to each one of these blessings from the Heavenly Father.

Both the Old and New Testaments are replete with **promises**. Focusing on them gives encouragement and peace, again often pertaining to eternal destiny, even to the rewards of the eternal kingdom in the New Heaven and New Earth. Notice that the promises require an action on the part of those to whom they are directed. There are nine directives to "overcome." The believer must also "be faithful," "keep [His] deeds," "not soil their garments," "keep the word of [His] perseverance," "hold fast," and "hear [His] voice and open the door." The promises are concentrated in Revelation 2 and 3, the seven letters to the seven churches, and in the last two chapters of Revelation which focus on the His future kingdom.

His promises are as follows, lifted out of context but in complete sentences. "To him who overcomes I will grant to eat of the tree of life, which is in the Paradise of God." (Rev. 2:7) "Be faithful until death and I will give you the crown of life." (Rev. 2:10) "He who overcomes shall not be hurt by the second death." (Rev. 2:11) "To him who overcomes, to him I will give some of the hidden manna, and I will give him a white stone, and a new name written on the stone which no one knows but he who receives it." (Rev. 2:17) "And he who overcomes and he who keeps My deeds until the end, to him I will give authority over the nations; and he shall rule them with a rod of iron, as the vessels of the potter are broken to pieces, as I also have received authority from My Father." (Rev. 2:26-28)

The "few ... who have not soiled their garments ... will walk with Me in white; for they are worthy. He who overcomes shall thus be clothed in white garments; and I will not erase his name from the book of life, and I will confess his name before My Father, and before His angels." (Rev. 3:4-5) "Because you have kept the word of My perseverance, I also will keep (safeguard, not prevent) you from (or during) the hour of testing, that hour which is about to come upon the whole world, to test those who dwell upon the earth. I am coming quickly; hold fast what you have in order that no one take your crown. He who overcomes, I will make him a pillar in the temple of My God, and he will not go out from it anymore; and I will write upon him the name of My God, and the name of the city of My God, the new Jerusalem, which comes down out of heaven from My God, and My new name." (Rev. 3:10-12) "Behold I stand at the door and knock; if anyone hears My voice and opens the door, I will come in to him and will dine with him, and he with Me. He who overcomes, I will grant to him to sit down with me on My throne, as I also overcame and sat down with My Father on His throne." (Rev. 3:20–21)

"And I heard a loud voice from the throne saying, 'Behold, the tabernacle of God is among men, and He shall dwell among them, and they shall be His people, and God Himself shall be among them, and He shall wipe away every tear from their eyes; and there shall no longer be any death; there shall no longer be any mourning, or crying, or pain; the first things have passed away.' And He who sits on the throne said, 'Behold, I am making all things new.' And He said, "Write, for these words are faithful and true.' And He said to me, 'It is done. I am the Alpha and the Omega, the beginning and the end. I will give to the one who thirsts from the spring of the water of life without cost. He who overcomes shall inherit these things, and I will be his God and he will be My son.'" (Rev. 21:3-7)

"And there shall no longer be any curse; and the throne of God and of the Lamb shall be in it, and His bond-servants shall serve Him; and they shall see His face, and His name shall be on their foreheads. And there shall no longer be any night; and they shall not have need of the light of a lamp nor the light of the sun, because the Lord God shall illumine them; and they shall reign forever and ever." (Rev. 22:3-5) "Behold I am coming quickly, and My reward is with Me, to render to every man according to what he has done." (Rev.

22:12) "And let the one who is thirsty come; let the one who wishes take the water of life without cost." (Rev. 22:17)

The benefits are tremendous, not to mention mind-blowing. Just reading these verses is a blessing because Yahweh is sovereign throughout the tumultuous future.   But most importantly, it underscores the consequence of understanding and obeying so that the right choices can be made to ensure one's eternal destiny and rewards.

The level of **praise** in the book of Revelation is phenomenal. The book of Psalms contains much praise but the details of heavenly praise in Revelation are unmatched anywhere else in the Scriptures. Praise of Yahweh in heaven must make mortal praise on earth pale by comparison. Human minds struggle to grasp the intensity, depth and breadth of praise in all heaven and earth for the Creator. Endless and indescribable numbers of saints and angels, the four living creatures and the twenty-four elders worship Him, but so does the altar in heaven! It truly must be a sight to behold.

Revelation begins with praise of the Messiah by John in the salutation – ..."to Him be the glory and the dominion forever and ever. Amen." (Rev. 1:6) In praise of Yahweh the four living creatures proclaim, "Holy, holy, holy is the Lord God, the Almighty, who was and who is and who is to come." (Rev. 4:8) Then in verses 10 and 11 the elders fall down and cast their crowns before the throne, saying, "Worthy are Thou, our Lord and our God, to receive glory and honor and power; for Thou didst create all things, and because of Thy will they existed, and were created."

Praise of the Messiah continues in Revelation 5:4 when John weeps "because no one was found worthy to open the book or to look into it." But the Lamb, standing as if slain, takes the book and verses 8 through 14 detail the heavenly praise. First, "the four living creatures and twenty-four elders fell down before the Lamb, having each one a harp and golden bowls full of incense, which are the prayers of saints." Praise proceeds as "they sang a new song, saying, 'Worthy are Thou to take the book, and to break its seals; for Thou wast slain, and didst purchase for God with Thy blood men from every tribe and tongue and people and nation. And Thou hast made them to be a kingdom and priests to our God; and they will reign upon the earth.'" Then John looks and hears "the voice of many angels around the throne and the living creatures and the elders; and the number of them was myriads of myriads, and thousands of thousands, saying with a loud voice, 'Worthy is the Lamb that was slain to receive power and riches and wisdom and might and honor and glory and blessing. And every created thing which is in heaven and on the earth and under the earth and on the sea and all things in them [John] heard saying, 'To him who sits on the throne, and to the

Lamb, be blessing and honor and glory and dominion forever and ever.' And the four living creatures kept saying, 'Amen.' And the elders fell down and worshiped."

After the seal judgments are described in Revelation 6, the 144,000 are introduced in Revelation 7. Then more praise erupts, as detailed in verses 9 through 12. "After these things [John] looked, and behold, a great multitude, which no one could count, from every nation and all tribes and peoples and tongues, standing before the throne and before the Lamb, clothed in white robes, and palm branches were in their hands; and they cry out with a loud voice, saying, 'Salvation to our God who sits on the throne, and to the Lamb.' And all the angels were standing around the throne and around the elders and the four living creatures; and they fell on their faces before the throne and worshiped God, saying, 'Amen, blessing and glory and wisdom and thanksgiving and honor and power and might, be to our God forever and ever. Amen.'"

After the trumpet judgments of Revelation 8 and 9, Revelation 11 tells of the two witnesses, whose resurrection is followed by heavenly praise. Verses 16 and 17 describe that "the twenty-four elders who sit on their thrones before God, fell on their faces and worshiped God, saying, 'We give Thee thanks, O Lord God, the Almighty, who art and who wast, because Thou hast taken Thy great power and hast begun to reign.'"

Revelation 12 reveals one of the reasons for heavenly rejoicing. After Satan is thrown down to earth, verses 10 and 11 describe a loud voice announcing that the "brethren" overcame Satan "because of the blood of the Lamb and because of the word of their testimony," proving that "they did not love their life even unto death." The very next verse states, "For this reason, rejoice, O heavens and you who dwell in them."

Revelation 15, along with Revelation 14, is a prelude to the coming bowl judgments and includes more heavenly praise for Yahweh. In Revelation 15:2 "Those who had come off victorious from the beast...," the tribulation saints, sing the song of Moses and the song of the Lamb, saying, "Great and marvelous are Thy works, O Lord God, the Almighty; Righteous and true are Thy ways, Thou King of the nations. Who will not fear O Lord, and glorify Thy name? For Thou alone art holy; for all the nations will come and worship before Thee, for Thy righteous acts have been revealed."

In Revelation 16, between the third and fourth bowl judgments, praise for these devastating judgments is described. Verse 5 says, "And I heard the angel of the waters saying, 'Righteous are Thou, who art and who wast, O Holy One, because Thou didst judge these things; for they poured out the blood of saints and prophets, and Thou hast given them blood to drink. They deserve it. And [John] heard the altar saying, 'Yes, O Lord God, the Almighty, true and righteous are Thy judgments.'" More praise for judgment is in Revelation 18:20. "Rejoice over her, O heaven, and you saints and apostles and prophets, because God has pronounced judgment for you against her." The "her" is referring to Babylon.

Praise for His righteous judgment continues in Revelation 19:1 – 7. "After these things I heard, as it were, a loud voice of a great multitude in heaven saying, 'Hallelujah! Salvation and glory and power belong to our God; because His judgments are true and righteous, for He has judged the great harlot who was corrupting the earth with her immorality, and He has avenged the blood of His bond-servants on her.' And a second time they said, 'Hallelujah!' And a voice came from the throne, saying, 'Give praise to our God, all you His bondservants, you who fear Him, the small and the great.' And I heard, as it were, the voice of a great multitude and as the sound of many waters and as the sound of mighty peals of thunder, saying, 'Hallelujah! For the Lord our God, the Almighty, reigns. Let us rejoice and be glad and give the glory to Him, for the marriage of the Lamb has come and His bride has made herself ready." So, yet another reason for praise is the joining of Messiah, the Bridegroom, with His believers, the bride. But above all, His Kingdom has come and that is worthy of the highest praise!

Chapter 8
Questions, Commands and Warnings

Juxtaposed with the peaceful reassuring nature of the previous section are questions, commands and warnings which also deserve a closer look. Any warning or command in the Scriptures should be given diligent attention, but the questions should not be ignored. There may be a blessing after better understanding all of them.

The **questions** in the book of Revelation must be there for a reason. A few authors have proposed that they point to important precepts. There are seven questions scattered throughout, from Revelation 5 to 18. As mentioned, seven symbolizes perfection. The mystery is why have them, what their significance might be and what their relationship is to each other and to the rest of Revelation, especially to those verses in close proximity to each of the questions. They inquire who, what, why and how long. Angels, martyrs, elders and humans are those asking them.

The first question is put forward by "a strong angel proclaiming with a loud voice" in Revelation 5:2, "Who is worthy to open the book and to break its seals?" Of course, this points to the

Messiah, the Lamb who is worthy because He was slain, as seen in verses 5 through 8. As all heaven erupts into praise, they exclaim in verse 12, "Worthy is the Lamb that was slain to receive power and riches and wisdom and might and honor and glory and blessing."

The second question, in Revelation 6:10, asks, "How long, O Lord, holy and true, wilt Thou refrain from judging and avenging our blood on those who dwell on the earth?" Verse 9 indicates that it is proposed by the martyrs themselves, or the "souls of those who had been slain because of the word of God, and because of the testimony which they had maintained." This question seems to point to the coming tribulation. Verse 11 relates that "they should rest for a little while longer," until more martyrs are added to their numbers.

The third question, in Revelation 6:17, asks, "Who is able to stand?" Verse 15 indicates that it is "the kings of the earth" down to "every slave" who are crying out as they hide in caves from the devastation of the sixth seal. It could be a rhetorical question or it could point to the 144,000 which are the focus of the next verse, in the subsequent chapter. Note the stark contrast between who is advancing the question and to whom it may point if it is not rhetorical.

The fourth question, asked in Revelation 7:13 by one of the twenty-four elders in response to John, inquires, "Who are they and from where have they come?" Verse 9 indicates that he is referring to those who are "clothed in the white robes, with palm branches in their hands," the great multitude, "which no one could count, from every nation and all tribes and peoples and tongues, standing before the throne and before the Lamb." In verse 14 the elder answers, "These are the ones who come out of the great tribulation, and they have washed their robes and made them white in the blood of the Lamb." So they are tribulation saints, possibly persecuted, as verses 16 and 17 hint.

The fifth question, in Revelation 15:4, asks, "Who will not fear, O Lord, and glorify Thy name?" His name, Yahweh, will be a central focus at the end times. Also in that verse is a reference to "all the nations [that] will come and worship before Thee, for Thy righteous acts have been revealed." Then the subject changes, so the question must point to the faithful nations, those that know His name. The question is asked by "those who had come off victorious from the beast and from his image and from the number of his name," likely the tribulation saints. It is part of their "song of Moses the bond-servant of God and the song of the Lamb."

The song of Moses is sung by the Hebrews after they cross the Red Sea. Highlights of it, from Exodus 15:1-18, include the following. "Yahweh is my strength and song, and He has become my salvation." (vs. 2) "Yahweh is a warrior; Yahweh is His name." (vs.

89

3) "Who is like Thee among the gods, O Yahweh?"(vs. 11) Another song of Moses, at the end of his life, is found in Deuteronomy 32:1-43. Most of it recounts their history, but at the end Moses proclaims, "Rejoice, O nations, with His people; for He will avenge the blood of His servants, and will render vengeance on His adversaries, and will atone for His land and His people."

The sixth question, in Revelation 17:7, asks, "Why do you wonder?" An angel recognizes John's perplexity. The subsequent verses detail the harlot and the beast that carries her. So, it seems to point to their beastly kingdom. Verse 7 even refers to it as "the mystery" and the remainder of the chapter seems to be quite the riddle.

The seventh question asks, in Revelation 18:18, "What city is like the great city?" In the midst of Babylon's destruction, "every shipmaster and every passenger and sailor, and as many as make their living by the sea," laments the fall of Babylon, which in one hour "has been laid waste!" (vs. 19) This question points to Yahweh's righteous judgment of a despicable system and a world taken in by it that did not repent.

Whether or not there is a connection between these seven questions or whether there is an overall theme is anyone's guess. It is definitely interesting to look at the progression. Note that questions two and seven similarly point to judgment but one pertains to coming judgment and the other is asked in the midst of judgment. Ultimately, though, the questions do seem significant.

Like the questions, there is quite a bit of diversity in the **commands** themselves and in who is issuing them. Some may be more important than others, but none more so than the exhortation to repent, which is made not only to the churches in Revelation 2 and 3, but throughout Revelation everyone on earth is admonished to repent and is given every opportunity throughout the judgments. "He who has an ear, let him hear" is repeated eight times. The gospels record the Messiah urging the same thing.

An amazing thing is that the negative "do not ..." commands often have an encouraging message. In Revelation 1:17 the glorified Messiah says, "Do not be afraid," to John when he "fell at His feet as a dead man." One of the letters to the seven churches in Revelation 2:10 urges, "Do not fear what you are about to suffer." In Revelation 7:2-3 "another angel ascending from the rising sun, having the seal of the living God ... cried out with a loud voice to the four angels to whom it was granted to harm the earth and the sea, saying, 'Do not harm the earth or the sea or the trees, until we have sealed the bond-servants of our God on their foreheads.'"

For a second and third time John falls down to worship the being before him, but now it's an angel in both instances instead of the Messiah. In Revelation 17:1, "one of the seven angels who had the seven bowls" says to John, "Come here, I shall show you the judgment of the great harlot." So it is this angel that John tries to worship and is told in Revelation 19:10, "Do not do that; I am a fellow servant of yours ... worship God." Then Revelation 22:8 explains that John "fell down to worship at the feet of the angel who showed [him] these things." In verse 9 the angel tells John, "Do not do that, I am a fellow servant of yours ... worship God." The very next verse commands John, "Do not seal up the words of the prophecy of this book." In other words, write about it!

But the opposite command is given in Revelation 10:4 when a voice from heaven tells John, "Seal up the things which the seven peals of thunder have spoken and do not write them." The speculation is endless on what these "things" might be and there's no way to know without divine revelation.

As seen already, the command to write was given to John several times. In Revelation 1:11 "a loud voice like the sound of a trumpet" urges him to "write in a book what you see, and send it to the seven churches." Later in verse 19 the Messiah pronounces, "Write therefore the things which you have seen, and the things which are, and the things which shall take place after these things." Throughout Revelation 2 and 3, John is again instructed what to "write" to each of the seven churches. Twice John is directed to write a blessing, once in Revelation 14:13 and again in Revelation 19:9, the second and fourth blessings. In Revelation 21:5 "He who sits on the throne" encourages John, "Write, for these words are faithful and true." It is quite apparent that Yahweh wants the world to know about the prophecy of Revelation, the one exception being the words of the seven peals of thunder.

The command to come is repeated at least a dozen times. John is told to "come up here" or "come here" three times. In Revelation 4:1 "the first voice which [John] had heard, like the sound of a trumpet" tells John to not only "come up here" but also that he "will show [him] what must take place after these things," i.e., after the seven letters to the seven churches. Revelation 17:1 says that one of the seven angels with a bowl invites John to "come here, I shall show you the judgment of the great harlot." Then in Revelation 21:9 "one of the seven angels who had the seven bowls full of the seven last plagues" tells John, "Come here, I shall show you the bride, the wife of the Lamb." Note the progression here.

After the two witnesses die they are summoned to "come up here" in Revelation 11:12. "They went up into heaven in the cloud, and their enemies beheld them." Obviously, this is a different circumstance than what John experienced.

Revelation 18:4 is a command that is also a warning. "Come out of her (presumably Babylon or whatever it represents), my people, that you may not participate in her sins and that you may not receive her plagues ..." and not be part of the devastation that follows. In Revelation 19:17 an angel standing in the sun cries out with a loud voice to "all the birds which fly in mid-heaven, 'Come, assemble for the great supper of God,'" one consisting of the flesh of kings, commanders, mighty men and horses; all men, both free and slave, small and great. It appears to be the aftermath of the battle of Armageddon.

The remaining "come" commands are either in Revelation 6 or Revelation 22. Revelation 6 contains the seal judgments. "One of the four living creatures [said] as with a voice of thunder, 'Come.'" Then the white horse "went out conquering." The second living creature commands the red horse to "come," the third living creature commands the black horse to "come," and the fourth living creature commands the ashen horse to "come," all of them causing much death and destruction.

Revelation 22 is the closing chapter. In the last five verses these four commands to "come" are really invitations, three in one verse and one in another. Revelation 22:17 says, "And the Spirit and the bride say, 'Come.' And let the one who hears say, 'Come.' And let the one who is thirsty come, let the one who wishes take the water of life without cost." Verse 20 adds, "He who testifies to these things says, 'Yes, I' m coming quickly.' Amen. Come Lord Jesus." This is the second to last verse in the Bible.

The remaining commands vary from giving instruction and inspiring praise to exhorting, but they still encourage. In Revelation 2:5 John is told to write to the angel of the church in Ephesus, "Remember therefore from where you have fallen and repent and do the deeds you did at first." Revelation 2:25 says, "Nevertheless what you have, hold fast until I come." In Revelation 3:2 John is to write to the angel of the church in Sardis that the Holy Spirit says, "Wake up and strengthen the things that remain, which were about to die." Verse 3 continues, "Remember therefore what you have received and heard; and keep it, and repent." Verse 11 says, "I am coming quickly; hold fast what you have, in order that no one take your crown." Verse 19 exhorts, "Be zealous therefore, and repent."

In Revelation 5:5 a strong angel orders John to stop weeping when there is "no one in heaven, or on the earth, or under the earth" able to open the book with the seals, or to look into it. In Revelation 9:13, after the sixth angel sounds his trumpet, "a voice from the four horns of the golden altar which is before God" commands the sixth angel who has the trumpet to "release the four angels who are bound at the great river Euphrates." In Revelation 10:8 "the voice which [John] heard from heaven" directs him, "Go, take the book which is open in the hand of the angel who stands on the sea and on the land."

The angel tells John to eat it. Then in verse 11 "they said to [John], 'You must prophesy again concerning many peoples and nations and tongues and kings.'"

The next verse is Revelation 11:1 when "someone" instructs John, "Rise and measure the temple of God, and the altar, and those who worship in it." Then verse 2 further explains that John is not to measure the court which is outside the temple. Measuring is often associated with judgment, but there is not agreement about the meaning of these divergent instructions for each area.

In Revelation 14:6-7, "another angel flying in mid-heaven" preaches an eternal gospel with a loud voice to every people on the earth, "Fear God, and give Him glory ... and worship [the Creator]." Why? Because "the hour of His judgment has come." A stern announcement and an ultimatum follow from two more angels. In verse 15 a fourth angel comes out of the temple, crying out with a loud voice to "one like a son of man" sitting on the cloud, "Put in your sickle and reap," because the harvest of the earth is ripe. Then in verse 18 a sixth angel, "the one who has power over fire," comes out from the altar and with a loud voice orders the fifth angel, "Put in your sharp sickle and gather the clusters from the vine of the earth, because her grapes are ripe." Judgment as never before is at hand – the devastating bowls or plagues.

Revelation 16:1 describes "a loud voice from the temple saying to the seven angels, 'Go and pour out the seven bowls of the wrath of God into the earth.'" In Revelation 18:20 angels proclaim, "Rejoice over her, O heaven, and you saints and apostles and prophets, because God has pronounced judgment for you against [Babylon]." In Revelation 19:5 a voice from the throne says, "Give praise to our God, all you His bond-servants."

Seven times, at the end of each of the seven letters to the seven churches the last sentence is "He who has an ear, let him hear what the Spirit says to the churches." In Revelation 13:9 it simply states, "If anyone has an ear, let him hear." These could just as easily be considered warnings, which bring up the next topic.

To continue the pattern, the **warnings** have a fair amount of diversity as well. Some are "woes" and one is quite a riddle. A substantial number of them are found in the letters to the seven churches, where repentance is the overarching theme. The rest of them center on either earthly judgment or eternal destiny.

In Revelation 2:5, following the command to repent, the warning is "or else I am coming to you, and will remove your lampstand out of its place – unless you repent." Repent is mentioned twice in that single verse. Verse 16 similarly says, "Repent therefore; or else I am coming to you quickly and I will make war against [false teachers] with the sword of My mouth." Verse 21 speaks of repentance and is followed in verse 22 with, "Behold, I will cast [false teachers] upon a bed of sickness, and those who commit adultery with [them] into great tribulation, unless they repent of [their] deeds." Verse 23 goes on to say, "And I will kill [followers of false teaching] with pestilence; and all the churches will know that I am He who searches the minds and hearts; and I will give to each one of you according to your deeds."

In Revelation 3:3 the command to remember, obey and repent is followed by, "If therefore you will not wake up, I will come like a thief, and you will not know at what hour I will come upon you." Verse 8 warns, "I know your deeds." Verse 9 says, "Behold, I will cause those of the synagogue of Satan, who say that they are Jews, and are not, but lie – behold, I will make them to come and bow down at your feet, and to know that I have loved you." It is not clear why these people claim to be Jews. Later, in verse 15, "I know your deeds" is followed by, "So because you are lukewarm, and neither hot not cold, I will spit you out of My mouth." Verse 19 continues with, "Those whom I love, I reprove and discipline; be zealous therefore, and repent."

To say that repentance is important to Yahweh is to understate the matter. It is paramount. Not only is repentance urged again and again, but an accounting of it occurs at least three times. After the sixth trumpet and second woe Revelation 9:20-21 says, "And the rest of mankind, who were not killed by these plagues, did not repent of the works of their hands, so as not to worship demons, and the idols… and they did not repent of their murders nor of their sorceries nor of their immorality nor of their thefts."

Then, Revelation 16:9 reports no repentance after the fourth bowl judgment when the sun scorches men with fire and fierce heat. In fact the response is to blaspheme the name of Yahweh. Verse 11 discloses no repentance after the fifth bowl judgment when darkness causes men to gnaw their tongues because of pain. Again "they blasphemed the God of heaven." And even after the sixth bowl (war) and the seventh bowl (earthquake as never before and 100-pound hailstones) "men blasphemed God" (vs. 21), so there must be no repentance once more. How heartbreaking.

Woes are a type of warning. The most well-known woes of Revelation are those that are also the last three trumpets. They are quite different than the previous four trumpets (one-third judgments). Revelation 8:13 announces these three trumpet woes with, "Woe, woe, woe, to those who dwell on the earth, because of the remaining blasts of the trumpet of the three angels who are about to sound!" Then Revelation 9 reveals the first woe and fifth trumpet locusts of destruction as well as the second woe and sixth trumpet gargantuan army of horsemen, while Revelation 11:15 relates the sounding of the third woe and seventh trumpet which results in a heavenly response.

Revelation 12:12 is after the trumpet woes and before further woes, but it may or may not be related to them. "Woe to the earth and the sea, because the devil has come down to you, having great wrath, knowing that he has only a short time." As mentioned already, this refers to Satan being thrown out of heaven after a battle.

The later woes continue in Revelation 18. Verse 10 proclaims, "Woe, woe, the great city, Babylon, the strong city! For in one hour your judgment has come." Verse 16 resumes with, "Woe, woe, the great city, she who was clothed [in luxurious finery]; for in one hour such great wealth has been laid waste!" Verse 18 follows with, "Woe, woe, the great city, in which all who had ships at sea became rich by her wealth, for in one hour she has been laid waste!" There are a lot of exclamation marks associated with these woes, and such repetition often indicates importance, or in this case, severity.

The remaining warnings are some of the most sober ultimatums of all. Revelation 14:9b-10 says, "If anyone worships the beast and his image, and receives a mark on his forehead or upon his hands, he also will drink of the wine of the wrath of God, which is mixed in full strength in the cup of His anger; and he will be tormented with fire and brimstone in the presence of the holy angels, and in the presence of the Lamb." Revelation 20:5 warns, "And if anyone's name was not found written in the book of life, he was thrown into the lake of fire." Revelation 21:8 further clarifies, "But for the cowardly and unbelieving and abominable and murderous and immoral persons and sorcerers and idolaters and all liars, their part will be in the lake that burns with fire and brimstone, which is the second death."

Revelation 22:11 is like a riddle. "Let the one who does wrong, still do wrong; and let the one who is filthy, still be filthy, and let the one who is righteous, still practice righteousness, and let the one who is holy, still keep himself holy." At a certain point no opportunity to repent appears to be left, though obviously there is a choice up to that time. Scripture clearly teaches free will but also that eternal destinies are final. The gravity is pervasive.

Revelation 22:18-19 is familiar to many. "I testify to everyone who hears the words of the prophecy of this book; if anyone adds to them, God shall add to him the plagues which are written in this book; and if anyone takes away from the words of the book of this prophecy, God shall take away his part from the tree of life and from the holy city, which are written in this book." Several Old Testament scriptures reinforce this precept: Deuteronomy 4:2 and 12:32, as well as Proverbs 30:6. It is very important to study all Scripture verbatim and in context. Bible classes, commentaries, Christian books or talks, and dissection techniques like this primer are all fine and good, but not enough. Believers must always daily go to the Scriptures. That is where they will find His Truth!

Chapter 9
Conclusion

Hopefully, it has been helpful to break down the details of Revelation in this way. But if not, it is imperative to search for another way. We all comprehend differently, so a particular style of learning will appeal to some and not to others. There are many strategies that can be used to acquire facts. A suggestion given by most teachers to their students is to find what works best for them.

The same advice given for studying any Scripture also applies to Revelation and related prophecy. Examine it carefully and prayerfully. Balance it with Scripture elsewhere. Be open for the Holy Spirit to reveal His truth, in His own timing. In addition, be aware that some biblical prophecy has a double meaning, pertaining to ancient times of the past and the end times of the future. In many places it is not clear where prophecy of the near future of John's day, ancient times to us, (Temple destruction, Christian persecution) ends and the much later end of times prophecy begins. Thus, prophecy can be tightly woven, adding layer upon layer of complexity.

Many, but not all, authors tie the Jewish fall festivals to the end times. This is a fascinating area to study and worth the effort. One can only be blessed a little more by a deeper understanding. It adds another layer of that complexity.

Pertaining to prophecy in general, keep an open mind. The reason that there are so many different interpretations or theories is that besides being purposely intricate Scripture is often poetic, repetitive, or general and sometimes vague. In addition, there are translation challenges. Theologians cannot even agree in which language the New Testament was written. One widespread theory on the rapture is based on the word "keep," translating it to mean prevent. The only problem is that the Hebrew word shamar or "keep" is usually translated to mean safeguard, thus supporting the exact opposite position. While there's no doubt that many theories or interpretations are plausible, there is also a reasonable chance that none of them is absolutely conclusive.

There are three questions that should be constantly asked when studying the different theories out there. First, what are the scriptural references to back up the idea? Second, how does that view balance with other related scripture? Third, are there competing or even opposing ideas just as plausible that also can be backed up with scripture? This requires honest analysis. Be wary of persons, whatever their credentials, who claim to have end times prophecy all figured out, if for no other reason than there are multiple well-qualified theologians with differing, even opposing, theories who fit into that category.

Most people interested in Revelation want to know the timing of events more than anything else. Revelation does not contain much "when" information. Many of the Old Testament prophets speak about the end times. The New Testament has important details, especially in Matthew 23 and 24, as well as Mark 13, because the Messiah is speaking. Keep in mind that trying to mesh all of the timing clues is an overwhelming endeavor. All one can do is continue to study it.

Some of the prophecy, especially about the timing, may not be clear because Yahweh probably wants believers to depend on Him for guidance. Maybe understanding requires prayer and contemplation, something unbelievers tend not to do even when they search the Scriptures. It requires His contribution, as does prophecy in the first place. "But know this first of all, that no prophecy of Scripture is a matter of one's own interpretation, for no prophecy was ever made by an act of human will, but man moved by the Holy Spirit spoke from God." (II Peter 1: 20 and 21)

Yet, there are three things certain about timing. First, the Messiah told the disciples, "It is not for you to know times or epochs which the Father has fixed by His own authority," in response to their asking if He had returned to restore "the kingdom of Israel."

(Acts 1:7) Secondly, Luke 12:40 says that "the Son of Man is coming at an hour that you do not expect." So, I guess that eliminates Dec. 21, 2012, or any other specific date. Is our modern calendar really accurate anyway? Thirdly, Matthew 24:36 says, "But of that day and hour no one knows, not even the angels of heaven, nor the Son, but the Father alone." But, we *are* to recognize those "tender leaves."

One more thought concerning time is worth mentioning. Many scholars, notably Albert Einstein, theorize that time on earth, as we know it, is very complex and time travel may be possible. In addition, time on earth is governed by a celestial clock with the solar system revolving around the sun. In heaven there is no sun so time is likely very different. Human minds struggle to comprehend all the intricacies of Creation.

In distinguishing between the different terminologies for this future period notice that plural and singular words are used. Are the "end times" the same as the "last days" and "those days?" Is the "end time" referencing many days or just one? Is the "last day" and "that day" the same thing as the "day of the Lord?" How does the "last hour" fit into all of this? The elephant in the room is the accuracy, or lack thereof, of the different translations. Yikes! How will the believer ever figure out this mystery? Well, this is another example of how much we desperately need to seek the guidance of the Holy Spirit as we stumble through the mine fields of prophecy.

Pertaining to Revelation specifically, pay attention to how the word "and" connects things. Take note of any possible progression. Always be aware of the significance of the numbers used. Watch the words "like" and "as" versus words that convey more concrete ideas. Be cognizant of what is described as a "sign" or "vision." Try to differentiate between what is best considered symbolic versus literal. Lastly, keep in mind that John is describing things that might be real, not symbolic, but were completely unknown to him. His difficulty in describing them may make them seem unreal and therefore symbolic. His descriptions have to be "interpreted" in light of 21st century technological capabilities.

Finally, and most importantly, be ready and be alert. Be ready by knowing what the Scriptures say about the future. Be alert to the signs of end times events, but also to false teaching and false messiahs. The gospels are full of the Messiah's concern that believers take heed, let no one deceive them or even tickle their ears, i.e., tell them what they want to hear. One of the absolutes in Scripture is that there will be a judgment day. Revelation makes clear that believers are to endure and NOT to take the mark of the beast for any reason. Reward for one's faith will far outweigh any earthly sacrifice or persecution. Believers must know the truth, persevere and be overcomers! They will be so blessed and all heaven will rejoice!

Made in the USA
Charleston, SC
06 April 2012